CROCHET FOR BEGINNERS

A Complete Guide of Crochet with step by step
instructions and Crochet Projects

MAMIE ANDERSON

TABLE OF CONTENTS

INTRODUCTION

The most common use for crocheting is, of course, to: Crochet aficionados have the goal of completing crochet projects, which often include the creation of items that are appealing, functional, or advantageous in some manner. Afghans, baby blankets, baby booties, hats, granny squares, shawls, handbags, tote bags, and other items are among the most popular crochet crafts. Many items, such as jewelry, socks, and even curtains, maybe crocheted.

Additionally, it is possible to crochet a variety of components that may then be used in other projects. For instance, crochet trimmings and edgings are popular crafts; you may apply them to objects that have been either crocheted or knitted, as well as those that have been stitched (including ready-made store-bought items.) You might, for instance, purchase some socks, towels, and pillowcases and then add a crocheted edge to each of these items.

Crochet designers often use acronyms to reduce the amount of space required to write their designs. To successfully read a crochet pattern, you will first need to comprehend the preceding information and get acquainted with the abbreviations contained in the design.

In most cases, the abbreviations may be found in a location that makes sense, given the context. Regarding the designs we have uploaded to our website, the abbreviations are located near the top of each pattern, just before the instructions. On our website, you can also find a comprehensive collection of crochet abbreviations that we have compiled.

If the pattern you use is from a book or magazine, you can typically find the abbreviations written somewhere in the front or back of the publication. If the pattern is from a website, you can usually find the abbreviations stated on the website.

Crochet and knitting are often confused by the general public. Several components are shared between the two crafts; for instance, knitters and crocheters use yarn to construct their finished products. Either method may make items that are functionally equivalent, such as Afghans, shawls, caps, and scarves.

You can tell at a glance whether a person is knitting or crocheting just by glancing at the equipment they use to create their project. If she is working with a hook, she is crocheting; if she is working with two pointed needles or maybe a circular knitting needle, she is knitting. In this book we will discuss and learn everything about crochet.

Chapter 1
INTRODUCTION TO CROCHET

Compared to other hobbies that involve doing handwork, like knitting or embroidery, modern crochet is a relative newcomer to the world of needle arts.

A hooked needle is used in the textile art of crochet to weave and loop together fibers (in most cases, yarn). From bags and blankets to toys and tea cozies, it's utilized to create a wide variety of products.

Contrary to knitting, its older and more traditional cousin, which dates back to the Middle Ages, crochet as we know it was created relatively recently, in the early 19th century, as a method to create a less expensive alternative to lace.

Crocheting gradually acquired popularity throughout the Victorian period, largely because Queen Victoria took it up. She is renowned for crocheting eight scarves for South African troops. Then, as we entered the 20th century, crochet was utilized to create whole clothes rather than only ornamental items like lace and little accessories like scarves and caps.

The heyday of crochet, however, was in the 1960s and 1970s, when it was especially popular for home décor items like plant holders and pillow covers, as well as clothing like dresses, blouses, and skirts. And as more and more people take up crochet, it seems like the bohemian/hippie style of the 1960s and 1970s is undergoing a kind of comeback.

1.1 History of Crochet

Lis Paludan has provided thorough historical documentation on crochet.

She combed the collections of European cathedrals and museums but could find no intact items that dated older than 1800. A similar lack of written evidence for earlier examples of crochet that can be recognized was also discovered by her. The Memoirs of a Highland Lady by Elizabeth Grant mentions shepherd's knitting (also known as slip-stitch crochet) from 1812. The oldest documented instructions may be found in a Dutch journal called Penelope from 1824, which included a discussion of the new method.

The slip stitch, or single crochet in British terms, was the first stitch used in crochet. In the colder northern regions, slip stitch with wool was utilized from Scotland through Scandinavia and into Eastern Europe before heading south via Estonia and Bosnia. Wool was utilized to create warm, weather-resistant garments. The most typical items were vests, undergarments, and mittens. To make wool mittens waterproof, the wool was often "filled" or aggressively massaged. Some of these things are still produced using the same processes and materials in a few locations today. When warm clothing made of thick, solid materials was needed, these locations had little incentive to make products with ornamental lacy stitching.

The warmer southern regions of France, the Netherlands, and Germany employed slip stitch to make personal accessories like miser bags, purses, and tobacco pouches in the early 1800s. While warmth was unnecessary, a sturdy cloth was required to prevent objects from falling from the bags. Early tobacco pouches, miser bags, and purses were made in rows or round using the back loop and several colors. The yarn had to be split at the end of each row because while knitting in rows; the task was always done from the right side. Slip stitch work could not be turned because the color work's design would be lost. Again, crocheters worked only on the right side while using the knitting technique known as working in the round, which was done as a tube. Either the open end was collected or folded in half and stitched.

In addition to collar and women's and baby's caps, designs for collars and hats were also published in German and Dutch within ten years after the first miser bag patterns (1835L).

The chain stitch and the single crochet stitch were incorporated to make these ornaments more aesthetically pleasing. As a result, crochet was no longer confined to solid tubes and straight pieces, allowing for more variation in form and design. The chain stitch makes it possible to create corners and chain meshes. Because chain meshes are adaptable, collar designs without body increases became common as the mesh curved around the neck.

However, these collars were straightforward, using mesh stitches for the body and chain "ladders" (single crochet in next single crochet after a few chains) for the edge. The caps were similarly basic. Adding more stitches in each round of single crochet, which had some height compared to a slip stitch, creating a flat circle for the crown (a technique borrowed from knitting). It was not possible to successfully produce increases using just slip stitch. The technique used by crocheters was the same as that used for slip stitch crochet, with the exception that brims were built using chains and individual crochet strands. The brim is knitted as a single rectangular piece on the right side solely, with the yarn being divided at the conclusion of each row.

Ten years later, in 1846 and 1847, Mlle. Riego de la Branchardiere released designs in England to replicate raised Spanish needle lace. This was the next significant invention. In addition to being three-dimensional, the lace was also worked through both top loops, higher stitches were used, and it was worked both forwards and backward. The basis for crochet as we know it now was established completely.

So how did it happen that in 30 years, we went from a simple slip stitch to intricate three-dimensional crocheted laces like Irish crochet? Materials, tools, women's education, and travel were all influences; they were all products of the Industrial Revolution.

Lace was entirely handcrafted before the Industrial Revolution and was a skilled craft performed by individual artisans. Machines that could swiftly produce large amounts of high-quality lace were created during the Industrial Revolution. Machines replaced people who manufactured lace for a living, and most people started doing it as a hobby. The final draft to be modernized was crochet lace, which didn't get off to a great start until the Industrial Revolution. In contrast to other kinds of lace, it could be produced fast and was the only kind that machines could not replicate. Elegant Irish crochet evolved into the pricey handmade lace preferred by the affluent; these crocheted garments demanded costs equivalent to almost $20,000 in modern money.

Humans utilize their free time to produce luxuries and works of art when their fundamental necessities have been addressed. For a long time, upper-class women pursued needlework as a hobby and a necessary skill. A working woman might claim a half day on Saturday and Sunday as leisure time, but a housewife would find a few spare minutes somewhere in the day. Whatever, the Industrial Revolution provided working middle-class women free time to utilize however they liked. Because crocheting just needed an affordable crochet hook and yarn/thread, it became a popular pastime for women of the upper and working classes. Crochet gained popularity when this was coupled with women's desire to be fashion aware.

1.2 Materials Used in History

A hooked needle, yarn, and thread were not always affordable materials for crocheting. Consistently high-quality needles were costly to produce until the Bessemer technique for large-batch steelmaking was invented in 1855. Wrought iron, which was softer than steel and simpler to deal with, was used to make the needle. The iron wire was sharp, trimmed to length, and had one end pierced with an eye. The punch also removed one side of the eye from a crochet needle. After being placed in crucibles surrounded by charcoal and burned to a white-hot temperature in earthen pits, the iron needles were gently cooled, utilizing the insulating properties of the soil. Low-grade steel was produced due to the iron being injected with carbon from the charcoal. However, the needles had not yet been finished. The needles' surface developed a hard scale during heating and cooling that needed to be polished off. After that, the crocheted needle was inserted into the handle, and it was finally ready for use.

By 1868, it was possible to make a needle and thread (needle and handle) out of a single piece of tempered steel rod, which sped up the production process (U.S. patent 76916). The price of hooks dropped, and they became easier to get.

The production of yarn and thread experienced developments of its own. The majority of bobbin and needle lace was produced with linen thread. Cotton thread was as costly as or even more so than linen before the cotton gin was created in 1793, and it was also weaker since the fibers were shorter. The cotton thread became affordable because of England's extensive textile industry, built on spinning and weaving cotton throughout the first half of the 1800s. The thread, however, wasn't usable for manufacturing lace until the invention of mercerization in 1844. The cotton thread became glossier, mold-resistant, and linen-like after being mercerized.

The growth of crochet depended heavily on the education of women, particularly teaching reading to women. Illiterate individuals who worked as professional crocheters created modest, straightforward objects from memory. We observed someone else learn how to crochet French buttons and Irish designs. Then, skilled crocheters developed a specific method and produced hundreds of the same buttons or patterns. At Irish crochet, those skilled in constructing grounds would merge the numerous motifs into a single accessory or item of clothing.

But since she crocheted as a pastime, she had to finish a whole item or clothing herself. A written design was required since the final result was more intricate than a single motif. The crocheter required reading comprehension. While most upper-class women had at least a rudimentary education for over a century, the Industrial Revolution's concentration of women in factories with free time gave many working-class women the chance to complete their basic education. Between 1850 and 1900, more publications were geared toward women, including books such as DMC Guide to Needlework and journals like Harper's Bazaar (1867) and Godey's Lady's Book (1830). (1886).

Like today's crocheters, those in the nineteenth century want an endless supply of fresh and unique designs. The first crochet pattern books weren't created until the 1840s.

Mlle. Riego de la Branchardiere of London was one of this era's most important crochet designers. She greatly contributed to the growth of crochet by creating fresh designs and clear instructions that she distributed as affordable books starting in 1846. 2 She taught "point, lace, crochet, tatting, embroidery, lace work, knitting etc." and was accomplished in many other sorts of needlework. Her crochet patterns were unique and often included concepts and design features from other needlework styles. Her published patterns for The Crochet Book, First Series demonstrate her prior work with crocheting point laces (also known as needle laces). She believes that raised Spanish needle lace is where Irish crochet originated in her Second Series, which replicates raised Spanish needle lace in crochet. Her publications were extensively used and helped promote innovations like turning the work, stitches higher than single crochet, and raised (padded) work, regardless of whether her claim to have invented Irish crochet is valid (and it very well may be).

The need for supplies and designs increased as crochet's popularity grew. Publishing patterns was seen as a fantastic marketing tool by thread producers like DMC, Coats, and Clark (Coats and Clark were independent firms at the time). Various pattern books that dealt with fillet (darned net) and other kinds of needlework served as one source for gridded designs.

1.3 What Sorts of Items Were Produced?

Early on, man—and it was the men's job—created his handiwork for functional reasons. To capture animals and ensnare fish or birds, hunters and fishermen used knotted strands of woven fibers, ropes, or strips of fabric. Other use included fishing nets, open-worked cooking utensils, and knotted game bags.

Personal decorating for special events like religious rituals, festivities, weddings, or funerals was included in the definition of handiwork. Some ceremonial outfits have a beautiful arm, ankle, and wrist decorations resembling crochet.

Royalty and the rich in 16th century Europe showered themselves in lace—trims, dresses, coats, and head-pieces—while the common people could only dream of donning such attire. Therefore, it may be inferred that crochet originated as a poor person's copy of wealthy people's lace.

In the Victorian era, crochet patterns were made available for items like flower pot holders, bird cage cover for visiting cards, wastepaper baskets (or "antis," covers to shield chairbacks from the hair oil worn by men in the middle of the 1800s), tobacco pouches, purses, and waistcoats. There was rug with footwarmers that card players could place under the table.

Women were crocheting cushions, coffee and teapot cozies, hot water bottle covers, travel rugs, chaise lounge rugs, sleigh rugs, and vehicle carpets between 1900 and 1930. During this period, potholders first appeared and quickly became a standard pattern for crocheters.

Nowadays, everything is possible. In the 1960s and 1970s, crochet gained popularity as a freeform art form, and now it may be seen in three-dimensional sculptures, clothes, carpets, and tapestries that show realistic and abstract patterns and themes.

1.4 Techniques from the Past and Present

It's fascinating to contrast traditional and contemporary crocheting techniques. For instance, it is noted in the Dutch journal Penelope from 1824 to 1833 that the yarn had to be slipped over the hook with the right forefinger while both the hook and yarn were held in the right hand. The hook is handled in the right hand and the yarn in the left, as right-handers do nowadays, in crochet manuals from the 1840s.

One should always "Maintain the same tightness, either crochet roughly or tightly, to generate an equal pleasing texture," as it was advised in a German journal from the year 1847. In addition, if you are not crocheted in the round, you should indeed break your fabric at the end for every row in order to get a more polished finish on the item you are crocheting. This gives the item a more professional appearance." Thank goodness, most designs now tell us to use both the correct and wrong sides of the cloth we are making. The turn of the 20th century saw the implementation of this modification.

The advice to maintain the same tension "seems to imply that crochet hooks were of the same thickness and that the crocheter was required to work in the right tension according to the design," according to researcher Lis Paludan.

Old pattern instructions from the middle of the nineteenth century said that the hook should only be put into the rear half of the stitch and that, unless otherwise specified, a single crochet stitch should be used. European author Jenny Lambert noted in 1847 that while working table runners and other items with single crochet inserted into the back half of the stitch was helpful, crocheting thicker-than-average soles for shoes and other items was only possible with single crochet inserted through both loops. Today, we naturally cycle through both loops until instructed differently.

1.5 Tips to Get Started

Building confidence is essential.

Giving someone confidence while beginning to teach them how to crochet is essential for success. We've discovered that explaining a stitch step-by-step at the beginning and even dissecting a straightforward pattern into its component stitches (for instance, chain and double crochet) are helpful. This is because it reduces a bigger project from requiring hundreds of stitches to only two basic, simple-to-learn stitches. The belief that you can learn to crochet and even do it fast come then.

Compliments as you go

Praise the student as you go as you start to teach them any of the stitches or patterns. They not only understand that they are on the correct path to mastering crochet but also realize that they are improving with each stitch and each practice session!

Tell your Story

Sharing your crocheting journey, including how and when you were taught, may be quite helpful since it demonstrates that you weren't born with the skill or suddenly realized you could crochet. We sometimes wonder aloud how other crafters do certain tasks, forgetting that learning and perfecting a skill might need a lot of practice.

Telling about your endeavors that weren't flawless or even ones that were a total failure also helps.

Be persistent and casual.

The person you're teaching will first struggle, just as it took you some time to get the hang of tension and stitches. They could pick things up much more quickly if you don't lose your temper or become angry than if you put them under a lot of pressure. Also, for this reason, informal classes function better.

Begin with a simple project.

Starting with a simple project can help them gain confidence more quickly and encourage them to continue

11

crocheting since they won't be as irritated or make as many errors. This is true whether they work in rows or rounds.

Instead of thread, begin with yarn.

Even the number 5 thread may be quite challenging to work with, and the thinner the yarn, the difficult it is to see, count, and maintain consistent tension. Aran or worsted weight yarn and the appropriate size crochet hook should be used for the first few lessons and the first project, at the very least.

Never begin with novelty yarn.

The ideal yarns for a beginner are not a novelty, even though they may be attractive and fascinating to work with. After all, you want the individual you're instructing to be able to easily see and count their stitches.

Chapter 2
BASICS TOOLS AND EQUIPMENT'S FOR CROCHET

We must educate ourselves on yarn and hooks before we can start learning how to crochet. We'll discuss the many crochet hook types, the different kinds of fibers used to form yarn, how to read a yarn label, the significance of gauge, and how to choose the best yarn for your projects in this chapter.

2.1 Hooks

Additionally, hooks with ergonomic grips are available. These are beneficial if you have arthritis or wrist or hand discomfort while holding a hook for an extended time. The majority of hooks are made pretty much the same way. The length of the handle and the throat—the distance between the head and the shaft—could be the determining factors. To help you understand the terminology used to describe them, below is an image showing the anatomy of a crochet hook.

A Tunisian hook is another kind of hook. This style of the hook, which is longer and often has a cable connected to the end to keep stitches, is used for Tunisian crochet. We suggest investing in a high-quality set of metal hooks in sizes E to K to get started.

Aluminum, steel, wood, bamboo, or plastic may all be used to make crochet hooks. To accommodate various kinds of yarn and gauge needs, they come in various sizes. The lowest size is 0.6 mm, and the largest is 15 mm or more. The length of the hooks is typically between 5 inches (125 mm) and 8 inches (200 mm). To assist you in holding it at the proper angle, the shaft beneath the hook may be flattened or cylindrical. To choose which solution fits you best, try out the various choices.

The diameter of the hook shaft is given in millimeters using the widely used metric sizing method known as the International Standard Range (ISR).

Steel hooks, tiny sizes for delicate work, and aluminum or plastic hooks, which are bigger and often termed wool hooks, were the two sizes used for crochet hooks before the adoption of metric sizing. It is helpful to know that U.S. sizes were used in the United States and Imperial sizes in the United Kingdom and Canada since you could have vintage hooks in your collection or want to utilize a vintage crochet design.

The table below illustrates how hooks named under various schemes may be misunderstood. Always take your gauge readings.

Thankfully, most hooks include a size indication on the thumb rest or at the base of the handle. However, if you come across a hook with no size indicator, you may be tempted to put it through a gauge check, a piece of plastic or metal with holes in it. The head won't fit through the right-sized hole if it is large, as with a round head. Try comparing the shaft size of the mystery hook to a known hook with a specified size for these hooks. Compare them by rolling them between your fingers.

The use of a crochet hook is rather simple. The grip or pad, which is an indentation in the handle of most hooks, is where you hold the hook while using it. The grip or pad you use to hold the hook is located within the handle. Thread guides and lips may be divided into two categories. Bates hooks are more angular than Boyes hooks, which feature a more rounded thread guide. Your choice of hook kind is entirely subjective. After using both, you can't notice much of a difference between them. However, some ardent followers swear by their preferred brand, so check them out and decide which one you like most.

You may wish to give Tunisian crochet a try as your abilities improves. A long hook is used in this kind of crocheting to retain the stitches. It resembles a long knitting needle with a crochet hook attached to one end. Additionally, Tunisian crochet hooks with a lengthy piece of metal or plastic used to hold several stitches are available. These have a hook on one end and resemble circular knitting needles. The size of an Afghan is one example of a very big project that uses circular Tunisian crochet hooks. Additionally, double-ended crochet hooks are available. These are used for more complex Tunisian-style crochet methods.

2.2 Yarn

Today, a wide variety of yarns are accessible. Almost every hue or color combination is available in various fiber kinds.

The yarn used nowadays is soft, practical, and long-lasting. Three types of fibers are used to make yarn: synthetic, plant, and animal.

Pet fibers

Wool, alpaca, silk, angora, cashmere, and mohair are animal fibers. The majority of animal fiber yarns need blocking. When you're done, dampen the cloth and wrap it in a thick, fluffy towel to eliminate any extra moisture.

After that, spread it out with your hands on blocking mats or another dry towel. Start by pinning the project, then shape it by working around the edges. Before you remove the pins, let it dry by relaxing and opening up the stitches, blocking. It also highlights the crochet's inherent beauty. Most animal fibers may be gently machine washed, but they should never be dried.

Natural fibers

Cotton, linen, soy, hemp, and bamboo are plant fibers used to manufacture yarn.

Cotton yarn absorbs water quite quickly, making it ideal for crafts for the kitchen and bathroom. Crochet thread for doilies, tablecloths and other lacy items is also made from cotton. Bamboo is great for lacy crafts like shawls because it offers fine stitch definitions. Clothing during the summer and warm climates should be made of linen. The fabric helps you stay dry and cool by wicking away moisture. The flexible soy and hemp yarns may be utilized for various crafts. Blocking is sometimes necessary with plant fiber yarns depending on the job you've finished.

For instance, after blocking, a bamboo shawl will change from a scrunched-up piece of cloth to a stunning work of art. However, carefully verify the yarn label. Most plant fiber yarns may be machine washed and dried without any issues.

Artificial fibers

Acrylic, polyester, microfiber, and other synthetic fibers are created from petroleum products. For a variety of crafts, acrylic yarn is a fantastic option. It comes in a huge selection of colors and patterns and is simple to work with and maintain. Various synthetic fibers are combined with other kinds of fibers to enhance longevity, ease of maintenance, and distinctive qualities like shine and glitter.

The majority of the time, synthetic yarn may be machine washed and dried without blocking.

Weight

Weights of yarn range from lace to giant. The various weights and the suggested hook size for each is shown in the following chart.

Yarn Weight Chart			
Weight	**Description**	**Recommended Hook**	**Stitches in 4"**
0	Lace	Fingerling, Size 10 Crochet Thread	Steel 1.6-1.4mm/B-1	32-48
1	Superfine	Sock, Fingerling	2.25-3mm/B-1 to E-4	21-32
2	Fine	Sport, Baby	3.4-4.5mm/E-4 to 7	16-20
3	Light	DK, Light Worsted	4.5-5.5mm/7 to I/9	12-17
4	Medium	Worsted, Afghan, Aran	5.5-6.5mm/I-9 to K-10 ½	11-14
5	Bulky	Chunky, Craft, Rug	6.5-9mm/K-10 ½ to M-13	8-11
6	Super Bulky	Super Bulky, Roving	9-15mm/m-13 to Q	7-9
7	Jumbo	Jumbo, Roving	15mm and up	6 or more

Yarns offered expressly for crocheting are often made of fine, smooth cotton. These yarns are typically identified by a number ranging from 5 (the coarsest yarn) to 60 (extremely fine yarn used for traditional crochet). The term "mercerized" is often used to refer to these cotton yarns; this indicates that they have been treated with an alkali to increase their strength and shine. They are perfect for displaying complicated patterns and other kinds of textures.

Fine yarns made from natural linen are also appropriate for crochet, offering the finished product a crisp appearance.

Traditional crochet yarns provide a finish that is harder and more tightly twisted, but pearl-cotton yarns, which are available for use in crochet, knitting, and embroidery, produce a finish that is softer and less tightly twisted.

They are produced in a variety of different thicknesses at the factory.

Yarns designed for smooth and firm knitting may also be used for crochet. These are available in several different weights, ranging from 3-ply (the finest) to 4-ply, double knitting and sport weight, all the way up to bulky weight. Cotton, wool, or synthetic may be used to make them.

Specialty yarns designed specifically for knitting, such as silk, glossy viscose, and metallic Lurex, may also be used for crochet. Steer clear of those with loosely spun texture since they could get caught on the hook more quickly.

It's a lot of fun to experiment with different knitting yarns, giving your work a new perspective. Be wary of any yarn that has a very densely packed texture. The patterns created by many stitches will be lost if the yarn is too complicated, and it may be difficult to perceive the structure of the stitches when the hook is inserted.

You may crochet with any material that is fine, flexible, and continuous; some examples are string (either natural or synthetic), raffia, and leather thonging. As an embroidery material, you may purchase a variety of exotic threads, such as metallic tapes. Beads and sequins used for crochet should have sufficiently big holes to allow the yarn to pass through them without difficulty.

Accessories

* To finish a crochet creation, you only need a few different accessories.
* Cut the yarn with precision with these little, sharp scissors.
* A tape measure may be used to check your gauge.
* Markers in the form of split rings may be used as counting assistance by being put onto a specific stitch or row. They may also be used as stitch holders, which is very helpful when working with various colors; the loop from the hook is put over a ring to secure it while you work on another area of the design using a different color.
* For holding your work while it is being assembled, you will need pins with big heads that will not vanish between the threads.
* Needles for tapestry work. This is the one that works best when it comes to stitching seams. They come in various sizes and have various features, including a big eye and a blunt tip that prevents the yarn from being split.

Gauge

Gauge measures the number of stitches and rows in a cloth swatch 4 inches wide. Always spend the time necessary to do a gauge swatch in crochet using the yarn and hook size specified in the design. This will enable you to determine if you need to adjust the tension or change the hook size.

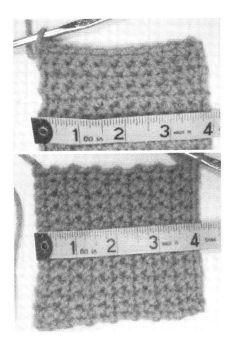

For instance, the sample seen above was crocheted with a size I/9 crochet hook and Red Heart Super Saver yarn, which weighs 4. A square patch of crochet fabric measuring four inches on a side has 13 stitches in each row and 15 rows. Check these measurements against the gauge provided in the pattern to ensure that the finished product will be the size you anticipate. If your gauge swatch is coming out too big, try crocheting it with a smaller hook size and seeing how it turns out. If the gauge swatch you made turned out too tiny, you could try crocheting it again with a larger hook.

Label of the Yarn

The yarn label is one of the most significant tools that you may use to assist you in selecting the appropriate yarn for your project. On the label of the yarn, you will discover information on the types of fibers used, the weight, the suggested hook and needle sizes, the gauge, and advice for caring for the yarn.

In this illustration, we can see that this yarn belongs to weight class 4, is made of acrylic, and that the hook size I/9 is suggested. If you use a hook of this size, you will get a gauge swatch with 12 single crochet stitches in a row that is 4 inches long and 15 rows in a square that is 4 inches long when you crochet it. This yarn may be washed and dried in a machine. However, the temperature should not exceed 104 degrees. There is no dye lot available for this yarn, but if there were, you would want to ensure that all of the yarn in your project had the same dye lot.

Skeins versus Balls

You may hear the phrases "balls" and "skein" used interchangeably. The yarn for a skein is drawn from the middle of the yarn, while the yarn for a ball of yarn is pulled from the outside. Because not all balls are circular, and some appear like skeins, it is essential to understand how to start pulling the yarn so that you do not wind up with a tangled mess. A hank is a loop of yarn; before it can be used, it must be coiled up into a ball.

If you attempt to crochet directly from the hank of yarn without first wrapping it into a ball, you will end up with a very untidy project.

Yarn Tips

Now that we've gone over the fundamental facts regarding yarn that you need to be aware of, we'd want to pass on to you some pointers I've picked up over the years.

Please read the label on the yarn and ensure you understand the information it contains. The yarn's label is the best place to get information about a yarn's weight, fiber content, suggested hook size, care instructions, and gauge.

If the yarn you choose has a number that corresponds to a dye lot, you should buy more of that dye lot than you need. It's not true that all yarns on the market now come in pre-determined dye lots, but if the one you're using does, it's best to stock up on more of it than you think you'll need so that the color doesn't shift when you have to add more.

You are free to use whatever brand of yarn you choose as long as it has the same weight and percentage of fiber content. If you only have Red Heart yarn, for instance, but the pattern asks for Vanna's Choice, you must ensure that the two yarns have the same weight. This will guarantee that your project turns out just as you envisioned.

Put aside for a later time the more costly yarns. If you come across some yarn that you have to have, go ahead and buy it so you can put it away for later use. For the time being, you should stick to yarns that are in the middle price range and are simple to work with and maintain.

Make it a point to avoid lighting up near your yarn supply or while working on your crochet project. It is quite easy for yarn to take up scents, and if you're producing something to give away, the last thing you want is it to smell like cigarette smoke. If you are given yarn as a present, and it has a smell, you may hide the yarn inside of a pillow case, tie the pillow case closed, and then wash and dry the pillow cover using the delicate cycle. In most cases, this eliminates smells from the yarn while preserving the integrity of the yarn balls and skeins.

2.3 What You Need to Have to Begin To get started

With crochet, you won't need many supplies. All required are a great set of aluminum hooks, a good pair of scissors, a tapestry or blunt needle, and some clip-on stitch markers. You won't be able to keep your yarn and other materials organized without a container. Depending on your preference, you may transport and store your works in progress in plastic tubs or large tote bags.

After you have gathered your materials and made sure you have a high-quality skein or ball of acrylic or wool yarn, we will begin learning how to crochet stitches and methods in the next chapter.

The Proper Way to Grip a Crochet Hook

There are two schools of thought when it comes to how a crochet hook should be held in one's hand.

The first is known as the pencil grip, while the second is known as the knife hold. When using a pencil holder, you will grip your hook like that of a pencil, as the name suggests. When you use a knife hold, you will grip your hook the same way as a kitchen knife. Both of these approaches are valid and result in stitches that are identical to one another. It is up to you to decide which grip you want to utilize. You should try both of them out and determine which one feels most comfortable to you. My preference has always been to hold the hook like a pencil. This is something that both my parents and my grandma instilled in me.

Nonetheless, Mikey from The Crochet Crowd utilizes the knife hold in every one of his video demonstrations; however, the final result is identical for both of us. Do not listen to anybody who tells you that the way you are holding your hook is incorrect. Either choice is OK; all that matters is that you go with your gut instinct.

Handle your Yarn

You need to wrap the yarn over my left hand and use your fingers and palm to manage the tension in the yarn. You "throw" the yarn over the hook by holding it with your index finger a few ways out from your hand and doing so over the hook. To maintain a consistent tension when crocheting, some people loop the yarn around their pinky finger and then bring it up between their ring and middle fingers. They "pick" the yarn with their hook and keep it in place with their index finger while doing so. Both approaches are valid, and you are free to devise your technique for holding the yarn if you choose. Maintaining constant tension while making it easy to work with the yarn should be the primary focus. It will become easier to work with the yarn as you progress in your crocheting, and you'll figure out the ideal technique to hold it all on your own.

Stitch Markers

Marking the beginning of pattern repetition, the beginning of a round when crocheting in the round, and color changes are all things that may be accomplished with the help of stitch markers.

You may get stitch markers in various materials and designs, from simple plastic clip-on versions to intricately beaded variants. You could even want to give crafting your stitch markers out of safety pins and beads a go and see how easy it is to do. It makes careful to use stitch markers that can be removed easily so that you don't end up crocheting them into your finished project.

A row counter is yet another helpful piece of equipment to have. You may refer to it whenever you need a reminder of whatever row you are on in the design you are working on. To obtain the desired appearance, many designs need repeated rows. There is a wide variety of designs to choose from while shopping for row counters. You may even use a piece of paper and a pencil to keep track of your rows by either writing down the row numbers or using hash marks. This can be done in either of two ways.

You may also consider getting a bag or a tote for carrying and storing your crochet materials.

Chain Stitch

The chain stitch is used for the foundation chains created at the start of a project and the patterns that are worked into the body of the crochet fabric. First, a slip knot has to be created and then placed on the hook. After placing the yarn over the hook, which will hereafter be referred to as a yarn over, draw the yarn through the slip knot on the hook. This is what's known as a chain stitch. To start the next chain stitch, you need to yarn over and draw the yarn through the loop on the hook. You should have 2 chain stitches at this point. Crochet chain repeatedly stitches until you feel confident managing the hook and yarn, and your stitches are smooth and even.

Single Crochet

The thick cloth results from using a single crochet stitch. Chain 12. Put the hook into the two chains down from the hook. It is believed to be the initial single crochet stitch in the row when the chain stitch is skipped. To complete the chain stitch, yarn over and pull the working yarn through the chain.

You should see two loops on the hook at this point. Turn the work over and draw the yarn through the two loops simultaneously. This is a single stitch worked in crochet. After yarning over and pulling through the next chain stitch, insert the hook into the next chain stitch, yarn over again, and pull through both loops on the hook.

Continue working your way across the chain by inserting a single crochet stitch into each of the chain stitches that are left. Turn the piece over after you have completed the final stitch.

To start a new row of single crochet, chain 1 at the beginning of the row. This is the initial single crochet stitch of the row, which will be tallied in the total number of stitches you need to make. Instead of inserting the hook into the base of the chain one, you will insert it into the next stitch. Repeat the previous step, yarning over and pulling through the stitch, then yarning over and pulling through the two loops on the hook. Work a single crochet stitch into each stitch until you reach the end of the row. The last stitch is worked into the foundation chain's skipped chain. This completes the pattern. The last stitch of the previous row must be worked into the first chain of the starting chain at the beginning of the following row and every row afterward. Always remember that the initial single crochet should be worked into the stitch immediately after the beginning chain of 1 and not into the base of chain 1.

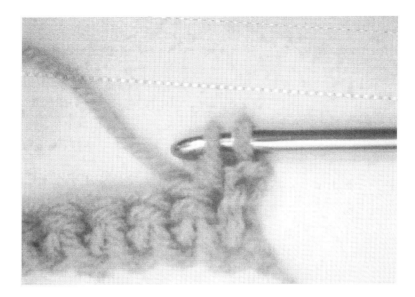

When beginning a new row, instead of inserting the hook into the base of the first chain, could you insert it into the next stitch? Wrap the yarn around and pull it through.

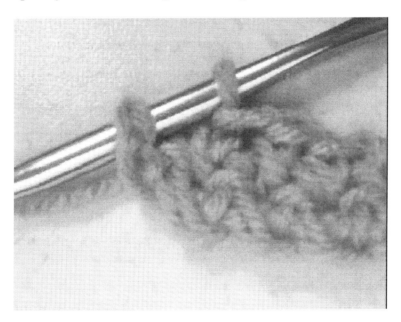

Put the last stitch into the last foundation chain, the first chain from the row before this one.

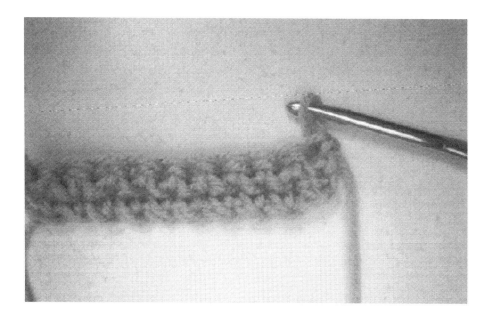

2 Rows worked in the single crochet stitch

Double Crochet

The double crochet stitch is the foundation for many other crochet patterns, including the shell stitch, the cluster stitch, and the puff stitch, amongst many others. If you start with a foundation chain, you should skip the first three chains, yarn over, and place the hook into the fourth chain from the hook. The initial double crochet stitch is regarded to be the first three chains that have been skipped. Turn the yarn and draw it through the chain before turning it again. You should see three loops on the hook at this point. Turn your work and pull through the first two loops once you've earned over.

Turn your work and pull through the two loops that are left. This particular stitch is called a double crochet stitch. To start the next stitch, you will need to yarn over and place the hook into the stitch directly in front of you. Turn the work and yarn over twice before pulling through the chain and the first two loops on the hook. Turn the work and yarn over, then draw through the two remaining loops on the hook. Make a chain of 12, and then practice your double crochet by working into each of the chains. When you have concluded, switch over your work.

Make three chains to start the following row. The turning chain is referred to as the three chains because they are thought to be the initial double crochet on the next row. Turn the work and place the hook into the next stitch rather than the beginning of the third chain from the hook. After yarning over and pulling through the stitch, you will need to yarn over and pull through two loops on the hook before moving on to the last two loops. Continue working across the row until you reach the last stitch, at which point you will insert it into the third chain of the starting chain. Every subsequent row should begin with a chain of three, and the very last stitch of the row should be worked into the third chain of the turning chain.

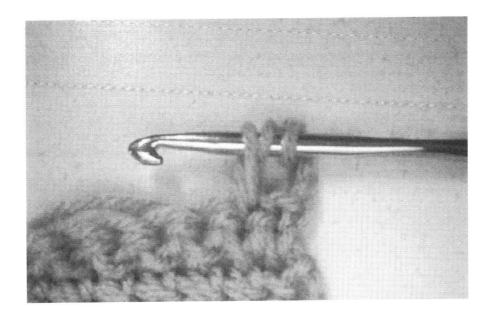

To begin, yarn over and pull through the first stitch. Then, put the hook into the next stitch and yarn over again.

Turn the work and yarn over twice, then pull through the first two loops on the hook.

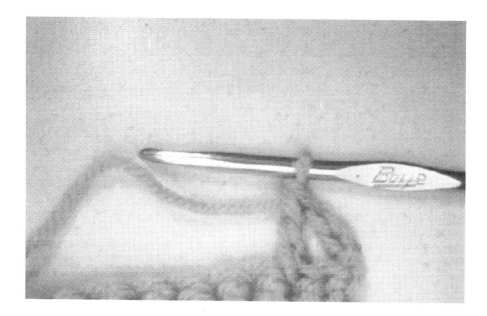

Turn the work with a yarn over and draw through the two remaining loops on the hook.

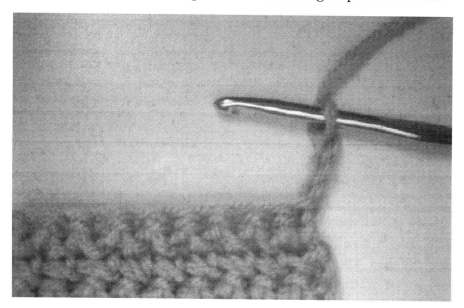

To start a new row, chain 3 stitches.

The half double crochet stitch

The single crochet produces a thicker fabric than the half-double crochet, which produces a less dense fabric than the double-crochet. By skipping two chains, yarning over, and inserting the hook into the third chain from the hook, one may begin to make a foundation chain. The initial half double crochet stitch is believed to be these two chains that have been skipped. To complete the chain stitch, yarn over and pull through all links. You should see three loops on the hook at this point. Turn the work over and pull through all three loops using the yarn over technique. The stitch that you see here is called the half-double crochet stitch. Start with a chain of 12 and work some practice half double crochet stitches across the chain. Once you have completed the last stitch, turn in your work.

To start a new row of chain 2, begin. This is the beginning of the first half of the double crochet stitch, also referred to as the turning chain. Turn the work with the yarn over and place the hook into the next stitch rather than the beginning of the second chain. Turn the work with the yarn over and draw it through the stitch.

Turn the work over and draw the yarn through each of the three loops on the hook. Continue to work across the row, and when you reach the end, work the last stitch into the second chain of the turning chain.

Treble Crochet

The treble crochet stitch, often known as the triple crochet stitch, results in a very airy and lax fabric. To begin with a foundation chain, yarn over twice, skip the first five chains, and place the hook into the sixth chain from the hook. This will create the foundation chain. The first stitch is regarded to be the first five chains that have been skipped. To complete the chain stitch, yarn over and pull the working yarn through the chain.

You should see that there are now four loops on the hook. After making a yarn over and pulling it through the first two loops, make another yarn over and draw it through the next two loops, and then make a yarn over and pull it through the last couple of loops on the hook. Start with a chain of 12 and work treble crochet across it. Turn in your work once you have finished the final stitch.

Chain five stitches at the beginning of each new row you work in treble crochet. These are the initial stitch, and they also count as the turning chain. Wrap the yarn around the hook twice before inserting it into the next stitch rather than the beginning of chain five. Turn the work with the yarn over and draw it through the stitch. Three times, yarn over and pull through both loops on the hook to complete this step. When you get to the end of the row, you will work the last stitch into the fifth chain that was skipped, which is also the fifth chain in the beginning.

Wrap the yarn around the hook before inserting it into the next stitch. Wrap the yarn around and pull it through.

To finish the stitch, you will need to yarn over three times and pull through the initial two loops on the hook.

Stitch in the sand

Utilizing the slip stitch allows the yarn to be moved to the appropriate location in the design. In addition, you may link a foundation chain with this stitch to crochet in the round. After inserting the hook into the correct stitch and doing a yarn over, draw the yarn through both the stitch and the loop on the hook.

The Back Loop Stitch and the Front Loop Stitch

If you examine a crochet stitch closely, you will see that the top loops create a "V" tilted to the side. In most cases, you will position the hook such that it goes under both of these loops. When working back loop or front loop stitches, the hook is only inserted beneath a single loop at a time. For instance, if you see blood written out in a design, you should start double crochet by inserting the hook beneath the back loop of the next stitch and nowhere else. The abbreviation for "front loop double crochet" is "flodc." Ridges are created on both the correct and incorrect sides of the cloth by the back and front loops.

Back loop stitch

Front loop stitch

Stitches in the Front and Back of the Post

If you look at a crochet stitch, you will see a post positioned behind the loops that make up the stitch. The stitch is worked around the post while doing a back or front post stitch; it is not worked through the loops of the thread. For instance, the front post double crocheted stitch (fpdc) starts with a yarn over, followed by the insertion of the hook from the front to the back around the post of the following stitch. Wrap the yarn around the post and draw it up to the same height as the other stitches in the row before yarning over again. Proceed with the stitch as you normally would. A front post stitch forms a vertical ridge on the right side of the cloth. A front post stitch will form a vertical ridge on the wrong side of the cloth.

To start a back post, double crocheted yarn over and enter the hook from backside to the front around the post of the next stitch. Then, pull the yarn through both loops on the hook. After yarning over, wrap the yarn around the post, pull it up until it is level with the other stitches in the row, and then finish the stitch as you normally would.

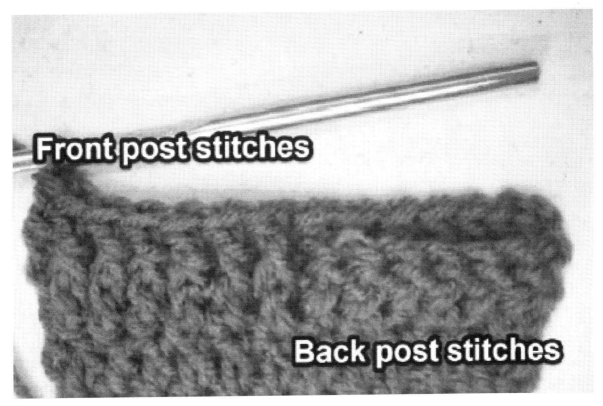

Increases

When crocheting beanies and hats from the crown down to the brim, you will need to apply increases to give the hat the desired form and bring it to the appropriate size. Crochet more than one stitch into a single stitch is all required for an increase. For instance, if the pattern instructs you to "2dc into the next stitch," you should make two double crochet stitches into the same thread.

Increases may be found in various designs, such as the peaks of a ripple pattern. They can also be used to shape clothes and serve various other functions.

Decreases

If you are cropping a hat from the brim up to the crown, you will need to reduce the number of stitches to properly form the crown. This is achieved by crocheting two stitches together to create one larger stitch. For instance, if you see sc2tog written in a design, you should combine two single crochet stitches to create one larger stitch. After yarning over and pulling through the first stitch, insert the hook into the stitch. After yarning over and pulling through the next stitch, insert the hook into the next stitch. You should see three loops on the hook at this point. To crochet the two stitches together, you will need to yarn over and pull through all three loops simultaneously.

A dc2tog, or double crochet two together, is created by inserting the hook into the beginning knot, yarning over and pulling through, and then yarning over and pulling through the primary two loops on the hook. The next step is to yarn over, pull through all three loops on the hook, then to yarn over or even pull through the primary two loops. Following a yarn over, the hook should be inserted into the next stitch. Finish the stitch by yarning over and drawing through all three on the hook at once.

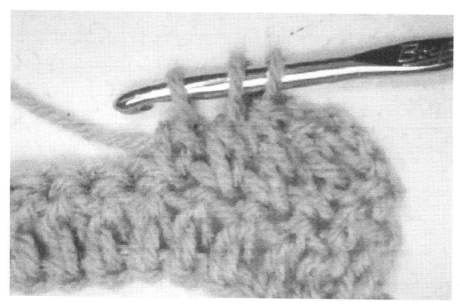

Crochet 2 stitches to the last loops

Dc2tog

2.4 Crochet stitches worked around a circle

In contrast to crocheting flat, you will need to crochet in the round to create items such as caps, cowls, and motifs. The act of crocheting in rows, both back and forth, is called flat crochet. You crochet around and around while working in rounds, just as the name suggests. Because you never turn your work until instructed by the pattern, the correct side of the cloth will always be facing you while you sew.

To begin, create a chain of 4 (or the number specified in the pattern). Slip stitch when inserting the hook into the initial chain of the project. This creates a ring and links the chain together. After you have completed the first chain of the starting chain, you will normally place the hook into the middle of the ring for the first round of the project. For instance, chain 3, and then double crochet into the loop for the number of stitches provided. If you work with a bigger loop, the design may instruct you to crochet the first round into the chain stitches. Always pay close attention to the points in the design that instruct you to begin crocheting the first round's stitches.

After you have finished one round, complete the circle by doing a slip stitch to connect to the third chain from the beginning (or the top of the starting chain). To keep track of the beginning and end of each round, mark the first stitch of each new round using a stitch marker with a clip attached to it. As each round is completed, you should shift the stitch marker to the first stitch of the next round.

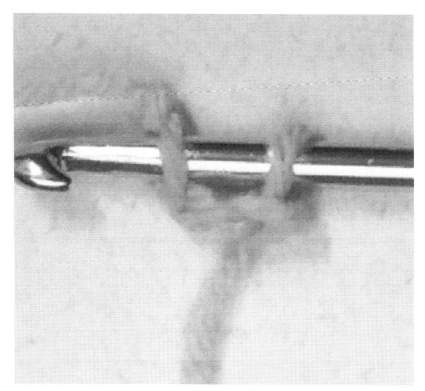

Chain 3 and slip stitch into the first chain to join and form a ring.

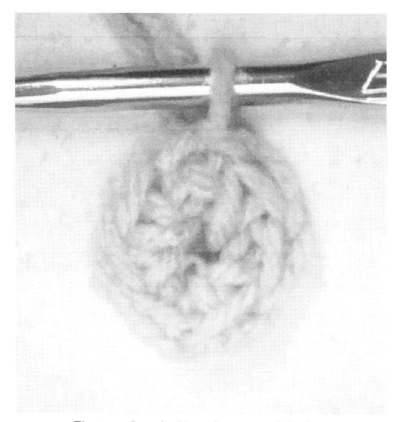

First round worked into the center of the loop.

2.5 Alterations in Color

Utilizing different hues is one method for communicating your creative side to others. Changing colors as you crochet is a simple process. Continue working in the previous color until the stitch is complete and two loops are on the hook. First, you will need to draw the new color through these two loops, and then you may work the stitches with the new color. My preferred method for incorporating the previous color into the first stitch of the new color is to put the yarn over the new color before beginning the next crochet stitch. This allows me to preserve the previous color.

This preserves the previous color and makes the new color more reliable.

Work the final stitch in the row or round until two loops are on the hook. Changing colors at the end of the row or round is necessary. Take the new color, and thread it through these loops in the chain. Now, crochet the first chain stitch of the new row while positioning the old color so that it is on top of the new color. The previous hue has been preserved. If you want to change the color of the yarn every other row, you should leave the previous color where it is and not cut it, which is also referred to as fastening off. When you get to the end of the row and come back across it, work the final stitch as if you were going to make it until two loops are left on the hook. Then take the previous color and draw it through that stitch. Make the starting chain of the next row with the color you just completed working with. Do this so the color transition is seamless. When you are going to be switching between two different colors, make sure the colors are carried up the side of the cloth. This helps the yarn remain tight and reduces the number of tails that need to be woven in.

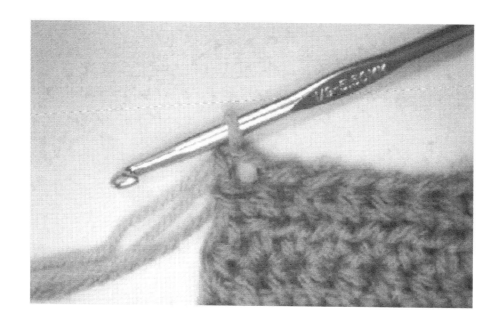

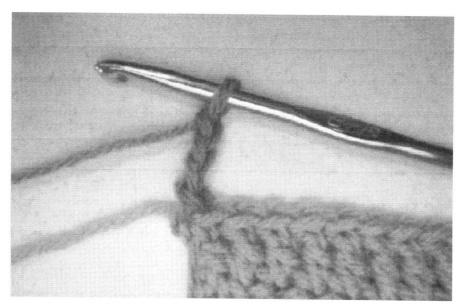

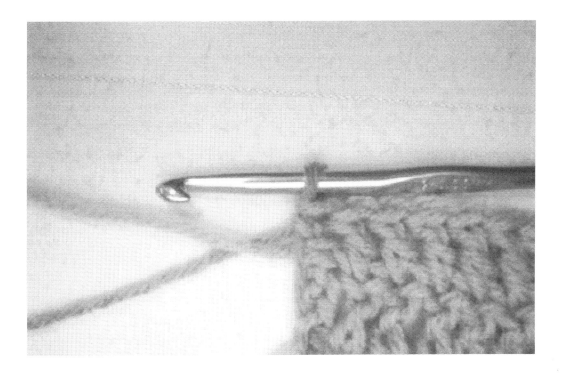

Techniques for Safely Weaving in Tails

When you finish working with the yarn and cut it or fasten it off, allow at least six inches to weave in. Bring the wrong side of the tails to the front of the cloth. Pass the tail through a needle with a blunt end or a tapestry needle. Weave the tail between the stitches for approximately an inch, going in and out of them. Flip the piece of work over and weave the tailback and forth in and out of the stitches for another inch. One more time, turn the piece of work and weave the tail in and out of the stitches for another inch's worth. The tail is held in place by this, preventing it from wriggling its way out of the work and creating more complications.

Weave the tail in and out of the stitches going three different directions to secure it.

Chapter 3
ABBREVIATIONS, AND SYMBOLS

In this chapter, we will go over the fundamental crochet stitches that are utilized in designs, as well as the abbreviations and symbols that correspond to those stitches. Written designs, diagrams, infographics, and schematics all make use of these acronyms and symbols in various capacities. If you currently know how to crochet, then you may use this chapter as a brief review to brush up on your skills. This chapter will introduce you to fundamental crochet stitches that you can use in any design. If you are just starting out, then this is the chapter for you.

List of Abbreviation

This table provides definitions for the acronyms that are used most often. In addition, some stitches and patterns call for the use of more specialist acronyms; these abbreviations, together with their explanations, are provided directly above the relevant textual instructions.

alt	alternate
beg	begin(ning)
C2B	slip 1 stitch onto cable needle and hold at back of work, knit 1, knit 1 from cable needle
C2F	slip 1 stitch onto cable needle and hold at front of work, knit 1, knit 1 from cable needle
C3B	slip 1 stitch onto cable needle and hold at back of work, knit 2, knit 1 from cable needle
C3F	slip 2 stitches onto cable needle and hold at front of work, knit 1, knit 2 from cable needle
C4B	slip 2 stitches onto cable needle and hold at back of work, knit 2, knit 2 from cable needle
C4F	slip 2 stitches onto cable needle and hold at front of work, knit 2, knit 2 from cable needle
C6B	slip 3 stitches onto cable needle and hold at back of work, knit 3, knit 3 from cable needle
C6F	slip 3 stitches onto cable needle and hold at front of work, knit 3, knit 3 from cable needle
CN	cable needle
Cr2B	cross 2 stitches back
Cr3B	cross 3 stitches back
Cr2F	cross 2 stitches front
Cr3F	cross 3 stitches front
inc1 K	knit into the front and back of the next stitch to increase one
inc1 P	purl into the front and back of the next stitch to increase one
K	knit
K2tog	knit 2 stitches together
K3tog	knit 3 stitches together
kwise	knitwise
LHN	left-hand needle

M1	make one stitch by knitting into the back of the horizontal loop before the next stitch
P	purl
P2tog	purl 2 stitches together
P3tog	purl 3 stitches together
P4tog	purl 4 stitches together
pwise	purlwise
psso	pass slipped stitch over
p2sso	pass 2 slipped stitches over

rem	remain(ing)
rep	repeat
RHN	right-hand needle
RS	right side
SKP	slip 1 stitch, knit 1, pass slipped stitch over
SK2P	slip 1 stitch, knit 2 stitches together, pass slipped stitch over
SK3P	slip 1 stitch, knit 3 stitches together, pass slipped stitch over
SPP	slip 1 stitch, purl 1, pass slipped stitch over
SP2P	slip 1 stitch, purl 2 stitches together, pass slipped stitch over
sl1	slip 1 stitch purlwise (unless otherwise instructed)
sl1k	slip 1 stitch knitwise
sl2k	slip 2 stitches knitwise
st(s)	stitch(es)
St st	stockinette stitch
T2B	twist 2 stitches back
T2F	twist 2 stitches front
tbl	through back loop
tfl	through front loop
tog	together
WS	wrong side
ybk (or yb)	yarn to the back
ybrn	yarn to the back and round needle (knit next stitch)
yfrn	yarn forward and round needle (purl next stitch)
yfwd (or yf)	yarn forward, or to the front (knit next stitch)
yon	yarn over needle
yrn	yarn round needle (purl next stitch)

The Same Repeats Itself

Denotes the beginning of a pattern repeat. [] Work the instructions in the brackets the appropriate number of times asked for by your pattern (] Work the instructions in the parentheses the appropriate number of times called for by your pattern * Denotes the beginning of a pattern repetition. * * Work the instructions that appear between the exclamation points as a pattern repeat as many times as the instructions for your design ask for you too.

Alternately, raise and lower.

When you see "2 togs" written out in a pattern, this is a decline, which is another name for it. You are going to work two stitches together at the same time. If the pattern asks for an increase, you will work two stitches into the area designated for one.

Chapter 4
STITCHING PATTERNS

4.1 Stich Library

Even experienced knitters will be tempted by the more than 300 stitch patterns in this book, even if many of them are simple to knit. You can choose from delicate, interesting, and fun, chunky textures; stitches that look best in one color and multicolor patterns; Aran, lace, and Fair Isle stitches.

Knit and purl, the two fundamental stitches, can be combined to create a staggering array of patterns and textures on their own. The most frequently employed, as displayed on this page, also offer the backdrops crucial for highlighting lace, cables, and other textural stitches to their greatest effect.

The hundreds of stitch designs developed over the generations are sampled in this section. Some of their names are well-known, while others may vary depending on where you are. It's intriguing how many references their visual connections or potential sources.

To get the most out of these stitch patterns, whether you pick the sporadic appeal of Simple Seed Texture stitch, the gratifying depth of Moss stitch, or the bulky texture of Mosaic stitch, use a simple, smooth, single-colored yarn and work with a reasonably tight gauge.

4.2 Knit and Purl Patterns

Knit and purl, the two fundamental stitches, can be combined to create a staggering array of patterns and textures on their own. The most popular, as seen on this spread, also offer the backdrops needed to highlight lace, cables, and other textural stitches to their best ability. The hundreds of stitch designs developed over the generations are sampled in this section. Some of their names are well-known, while others may vary depending on where you are. It's intriguing how many references their visual connections or potential sources. To get the most out of these stitch patterns, whether you pick the sporadic appeal of Simple Seed Texture stitch, the gratifying depth of Moss stitch, or the bulky texture of Mosaic stitch, use a simple, smooth, single-colored yarn and work with a reasonably tight gauge.

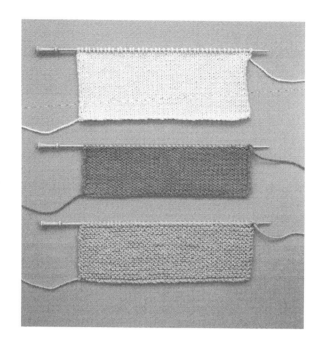

Stich STOCKINETTE (top section of picture)

STOCKINETTE stitch in reverse (middle section of picture)

STITCH GARTER (bottom section of picture)

Stich STOCKINETTE

Any amount of stitches

1st row: (RS) K.

Row 2: P.

Repeat those two rows.

STOCKINETTE stitch, reversed, any number of stitches

Row 1: P (RS)

Row 2: K.

Repeat those two rows.

STITCH GARTER (reversible)

any amount of stitches

K in every row.

SEED TEXTURE thread, SIMPLE (top section of picture)

DARK BROADCLOTH (middle section of picture)

SEED stitch, basic (bottom section of picture)

Multiples of 4 stitches + 1 in the SIMPLE SEED TEXTURE stitch

Row 1: P1, K3, P1, rep through the end (RS).

Row 2: P.

Row 3: K.

Row 4: P.

K2, P1, K3, P1, repeat from last 2 stitches, K2, P1. Row 5.

Row 6: P.

Row 7: K.

Row 8: P.

Repeat these 8 rows.

DARK BROADCLOTH

12 stitch multiples plus 1

Row 1: K1, P1, K9, P1, repeat from first stitch to last, K1.

Row 2: From beginning to conclusion, repeat K1, P1, K1, P7, K1, P1, K1.

Row 3: K1, P1, K5, P1, K1, P1, rep from first stitch to last, K1.

Row 4: K1, (P1, K1) twice, P3, K1, P1, K1, P2, repeat.

K3, P1, (K1, P1) three times, K2, and then K1 to complete the fifth row.

Row 6: P1, P3, K1, twice (P1, K1), P4, repeat from beginning to end.

K5, P1, K1, P1, K4, rep from first stitch to last, K1. Row 7.

As in row 6, row 8.

As row 5, row 9, and row 4, respectively.

As in row 3, row 11.

Row 12: From the beginning, repeat K1, P1, K1, P7, K1, P1, K1.

Do these 12 rows again.

SEED stitch, basic (BRITISH or IRISH MOSS stitch) (reversible)

2 st. multiples

K1, P1; repeat from beginning to end.

P1, K1, repeat along the row two.

Repeat those two rows.

two-stitch multiples plus one

K1, P1, K1, repeat from beginning to end.

Row 2: P1, K1, P1, continue to the end.

Repeat those two rows.

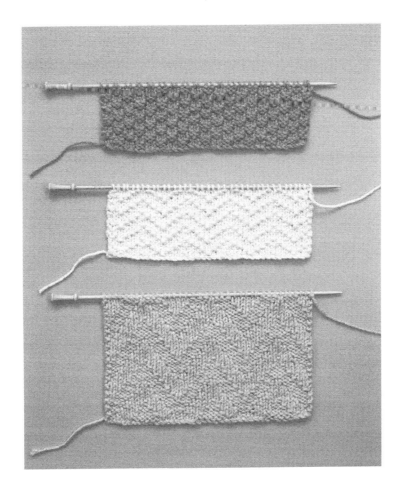

MOSS stitch TWICE (top section of picture)

stitched in CHEVRON SEED (middle section of picture)

CHEVRON pattern, DEEP (bottom section of picture)

MOSS stitch TWICE (reversible)

Numerous 4 stitches plus two

rows one: K2, P2, repeat from last two stitches, K2.

Row 2: K2, P2, P2, rep from previous two stitches.

As in row 2, row 3.

As in row 1, row 4.

Repeat these 4 rows.

Repeat these 4 rows.

Stitched in CHEVRON SEED

8-stitch multiples

(RS) P1, K3, repeat from beginning to end.

Row 2: K1, P5, K1, P1, continue to the finish.

Row 3: From starting to conclusion, perform K2, P1, K3, P1, and K1.

Row 4: P2, K1, P1, P3, repeat from beginning to end.

Repeat these 4 rows.

CHEVRON pattern, DEEP (reversible)

sts in multiples of 12

K3, P5, K3, P1, repeat in row one.

Row 2: From beginning to conclusion, K1, P3, K5, P3.

P1, K3, P3, repeat the last five stitches, K3, P2, P1.

Row 4: K2, P3, K3, P3, repeat till the final stitch, then K1.

P2, K3, P1, K3, P3, from beginning to conclusion, row 5.

Row 6: Repeat K3, P3, K1, P3, and K2 from beginning to end.

P3, K5, P3, K1, repeat for row 7

Row 8: P1, K3, P5, K3, continue till the end.

Row 9: K1, P3, K3, repeat from the last 5 stitches, P3, K2, and so on.

P2, K3, P3, K3, repeat till the final stitch, P1, row 10.

Row 11: From the beginning, repeat K2, P3, K1, P3, and K3.

P3, K3, P1, K3, P2, repeat till the end of row 12.

Do these 12 rows again.

STITCH DIAGONAL SEED (top section of picture)

Checkerboard RIB (middle section of the image)

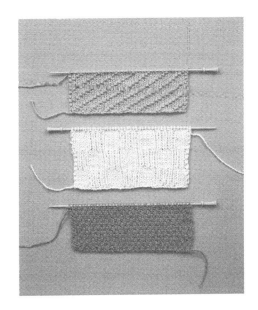

STITCH DIAGONAL SEED (top section of picture)

Checkerboard RIB (middle section of image)

Stitch MOSS (bottom area of picture)

Multiples of 5 stitches in DIAGONAL SEED stitch

Row 1: K4, P1, rep through the end (RS).

Row 2: P1, K1, P3, continue to the end.

Row 3: K2, P1, K2, continue to the end.

Row 4: P3, K1, P1, continue to the end.

Row 5: P1, K4, repeat from the beginning.

K1, P4, and so on for Row 6.

K3, P1, K1, repeat from the beginning of row 7

Row 8: P2, K1, P2, continue till the end.

K1, P1, K3, repeat from beginning to end.

P4, K1, repeat for 10 rows.

Ten rows of repetitions.

Checkerboard RIB

Numerous 13-st stitches

Row 1: K5, P1, K1, repeat from beginning to end (RS).

Row 2: (P1, K1, P5, rep from beginning to end)

3, 5, and 7: The same as row 1.

Row 2 applies to rows 4, 6, and 8.

Row 9: K1, P1, K5, repeat from beginning to end.

Row 10: P5, (KI, P1) four times; rep all the way through.

11, 13, and 15: The same as row 1.

Row 2 applies to rows 12, 14, and 16.

Do these 16 rows again.

Stitch MOSS (reversible)

2 st. multiples

K1, P1; repeat from beginning to end.

Like row 1, row 2.

Row 3: P1, K1, repeat from the beginning.

As in row 3, row 4.

Repeat these 4 rows.

Two-stitch multiples plus one

Row 1: K1, P1, repeat from the first stitch to the last, K1.

P1, K1, repeat till the final stitch, P1; row 2.

As in row 2, row 3.

As in row 1, row 4.

Repeat these 4 rows.

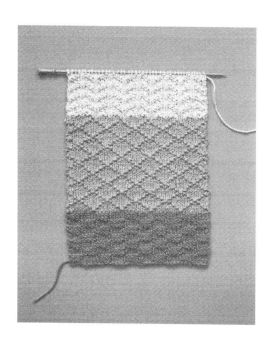

SMALL ARCHER stitch (top section of picture)

DARK DIAMOND brocade (middle section of picture)

QUAD-STITCH test (bottom section of picture)

SMALL ARCHER stitch

8-stitch multiples plus one

Row 1: K2, P2, K1, P2, K3, P2, K1, P2, rep from the first stitch to the last two stitches, K2.

P3, K1, P1, K1, P5, K1, P1, K1, repeat from last 3 stitches, P3. Row 2:

Row 3: From the beginning, repeat K1, P1, K5, P1, K1.

Row 4: From the beginning, repeat P1, K2, P3, K2, and P1.

Repeat these 4 rows.

Repeat these 4 rows.

DARK DIAMOND brocade

8-stitch multiples

Row 1: P1, K7, repeat from beginning to end.

Row 2: K1, P5, K1, P1, continue to the finish.

Row 3: From starting to conclusion, perform K2, P1, K3, P1, and K1.

Row 4: P2, K1, P1, P3, repeat from beginning to end.

K4, P1, K3, repeat from the beginning of row 5

As in row 4, row 6.

As in row 3, row 7.

As in row 2, row 8.

Repeat these 8 rows.

QUAD-STITCH test (reversible)

8-stitch multiples

K4, P4, repeat on rows 1, 2, and 3 to the end.

P4, K4, rep from the beginning for Rows 4, 5, and 6.

Repetition: 6 rows.

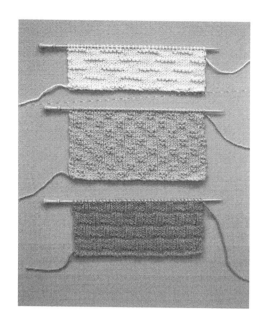

STITCH HORIZONTAL DASH (top section of picture)

Check the STOCKINETTE stitch (middle section of picture)

STITCH BASKET (bottom area of view)

STITCH: HORIZONTAL DASH Multiples of 10 stitches

(RS) K4, P6, rep from beginning to conclusion.

P on row 2 and every WS row.

Row 3: K.

P5, K4, P1, repeat for the entire row.

Row 7: K.

Row 8: P.

Repeat these 8 rows.

STITCHER STITCH check

8-stitch multiples

(RS) P2, K4, rep from beginning to conclusion.

Row 2: P.

As in row 1, row 3.

Row 4: P.

K3, P2, K4, repeat the previous three stitches, P2, K1 in row 5.

Row 6: P.

As row 5, row 7.

Row 8: P.

Repeat these 8 rows.

Multiples of 6 stitches in BASKET stitch

1st row: (RS) K.

Row 2: P.

Row 3: K1, P4, K1, continue to the end.

Row 4: P1, K4, P1, continue to the end.

As in row 3, row 5.

As in row 4, row 6.

Row 7: K.

Row 8: P.

Row 9: From the beginning, repeat P2, K2, P2.

K2, P2, K2, repeat from beginning to end.

Like row 9 and row 11.

the same as row 10.

Do these 12 rows again.

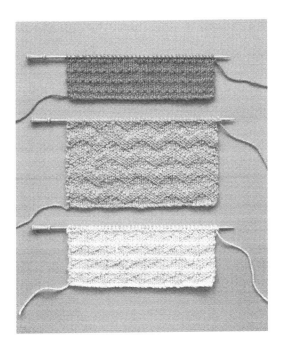

Spanish stitch (top section of picture)

VERTICAL WELT stitch (middle section of the image)

Pentagram stitch (bottom area of the image)

ANDALUSIAN stitch

2 st. multiples

1st row: (RS) K.

Row 2: P.

K1, P1, repeat in row 3 to the end.

Row 4: P.

Repeat these 4 rows.

Repeat these 4 rows.

WAVED WELT stitch (reversible)

8-stitch multiples plus one

Row 1: P1, K7, rep from the first stitch to last, P1. (RS)

Row 2: P5, K2, K2,*P5, K3, repeat from * to the previous 7 stitches.

P3, *K3, P5, rep from * to the final 6 stitches, K3, P3, in row three.

K4, P1, K7, repeat from last 5 stitches, K4, P1, K4 in row 4.

*K1, P7, repeat from * until the last stitch, K1. Row 5.

P2, *K5, P3, rep from * until the final 7 stitches, K5, P2. Row 6.

K3, P3, K5, repeat from * to the last 6 stitches, K3, P3, K3.

P4, *K1, P7, repeat from * to final 5 stitches, K1, P4, row 8.

Repeat these 8 rows.

PENNANT stitch

5 st. multiples

1st row: (RS) K.

Row 2: From beginning to conclusion, K1, P4.

Row 3: From *K3, P2, repeat till the finish.

As in row 3, row 4.

As in row 2, row 5.

Row 6: K.

Repetition: 6 rows.

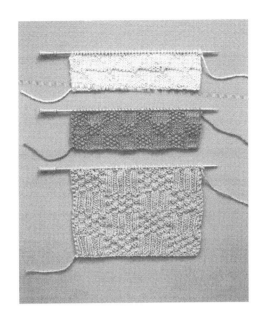

FIGURE 8 stitch (top section of picture)

SEEK SEEDS (middle section of the image)

STITCH MOSAIC (bottom area of view)

Multiples of 8 stitches plus 1 for the PYRAMID stitch

(RS) K1, P7, *K1, K1, repeat from * to last stitch.

P1, *K7, P1, repeat from * to the end of row 2.

Row three: *K2, P5, K1, repeat from * until the final stitch, K1.

P1, *P1, K5, P2, repeat from * until the end for row 4.

K3, P3, K2, repeat from * to the last stitch, K1, in row five.

P1, *P2, K3, P3, repeat from * until the end for row 6.

Row 7: K4, P1, K3, repeat from the first stitch to the last, K1.

P1, *P3, K1, P4, repeat from * until the end of row 8.

Row 9: P4, K1, P3, and so on till the last stitch, P1.

K1, *K3, P1, K4, repeat from * until the end of the row.

Row 11: P3, K3, P2, repeat from * to the last stitch, then P1.

K1, *K2, P3, K3, repeat from * until the end of row 12.

P2, K5, P1, repeat from * to last stitch, P1, in row 13.

K1, *K1, P5, K2, repeat from * until the end for row 14.

Row 15: P1, K7, repeat from the first stitch to last, P1.

K1, *P7, K1, repeat from * to end for row 16.

Do these 16 rows again.

Multiples of 10 sts plus 5 for a SEEDED check

Row 1: (RS) *K5, (P1, K1) twice, P1, rep * till last 5 stitches, K5.

P5, *(P1, K1) twice, P6, repeat from * until the end of the row.

As in rows 1: Rows 3 and 5.

As in rows 4 and 6,

(K1, P1) K1, P5, repeat from * across the last five stitches, (K1, P1) twice, K1. Row 7:

Row 8: (K1, P1) twice, K6, *(K1, P1) twice, K1, rep from * until the last 5 stitches.

As in row 1, row 9.

As in row 2, row 10.

As in row 1, row 11.

As in row 2, row 12.

Do these 12 rows again.

STITCH MOSAIC

20-st. multiples + 10.

P2, K2, rep from first two stitches to final two, P2 (RS).

Row two: K2, P2, repeat from last two stitches, K2.

(K2, P2) twice, *K4, P2, K2, P2, rep from * to the last two stitches, K2. Row 3.

Row 4: P2, K2, P4, K2, P2, K2, repeat from * to the last 2 stitches, P2.

Repeat rows 1-4 in rows 5-8.

Repeat rows 1-2 in rows 9 and 10.

As in row 2, row 11.

As in row 1, row 12.

As in row 3, row 13.

As in row 4, row 14.

Repeat rows 11−14 in rows 15−18.

Repeat rows 11−12 in rows 19 and 20.

20 rows of repetitions.

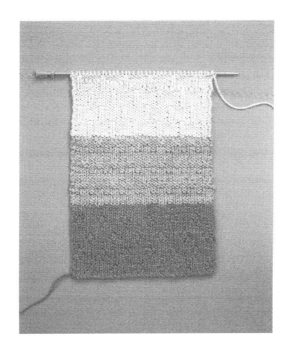

CATERPILLAR stitch, vertical (top section of picture)

Stitched by HARRIS (middle section of image)

STITCH DIAMOND SEED (bottom area of picture)

Multiples of 6 stitches plus 2 for the VERTICAL CATERPILLAR stitch

Row 1: P2, *K1, P5, repeat from * to the end (RS).

Row 2: K5, P1, repeat from * to the final two stitches, K2.

As in row 1, row 3.

As in row 2, row 4.

as in row 1, row 5.

As in row 2, row 6.

P5, K1, repeat from the last two stitches, K2, in row 7.

K2, P1, K5, repeat from beginning to end.

As in row 7, row 9.

As in row 8, row 10.

As in row 7, row 11.

As in row 8, row 12.

Do these 12 rows again.

stitched by HARRIS (reversible)

4 st. multiples

K2, P2, and repeat for one row.

Like row 1, row 2.

Row 3: K.

Row 4: P.

The same as rows 5 and 6.

Row 7: P.

Row 8: K.

Repeat these 8 rows.

Multiples of 6 stitches in DIAMOND SEED stitch

Row 1: K1, P1, K4 (RS) from beginning to end.

Row 2: P4, K1, P1, continue to the end.

P1, K1, P1, K3, repeat from beginning to end.

P3, K1, P1, K1, repeat from the beginning of row 4

as in row 1, row 5.

As in row 2, row 6.

K4, P1, K1, repeat from the beginning of row 7

P1, K1, P4, repeat from beginning to end.

Row 9: From beginning to conclusion, repeat K3, P1, K1, P1.

Row 10: From starting to close, repeat K1, P1, K1, P3.

As in row 7, row 11.

As in row 8, row 12.

Do these 12 rows again.

Knit and purl panels

The robust vertical panels of the gansey, the customary working outfit of nineteenth-century British fisherman, are made with a simple combination of knit and purl stitches. The gansey stitch designs were first developed in fishing settlements along the coasts of the Channel Islands and up the east coast of Britain to Scotland. They are now highly prized on a global scale. On the sample to the right, the Tree of Life and Basic Seed stitch panels show how just two stitch patterns may provide a stunning result.

Originally, these stitch patterns were not formally recorded; they were passed down from knitter to knitter. Although designs like the Tree of Life and Marriage Lines have greater symbolic meanings, they were frequently inspired by commonplace objects like fishing nets, anchors, herringbones, and lightning.

Ganseys were traditionally made of navy-blue worsted wool and knit tightly to keep the elements away. Denim cotton is a common option, although much simple wool and cotton yarns today display the stitch patterns effectively.

Panel for basic seed stitching (outer and middle sections of picture)

meeting for TREE OF LIFE (main sections of image)

Basic Seed Stitch Panel (British or Irish Moss Stitch) (reversible)

2 st. multiples

K1, P1; repeat from beginning to end.

P1, K1, repeat along the row two.

Repeat those two rows.

two-stitch multiples plus one

two-stitch multiples plus one

Row 1: K1, P1, repeat from first stitch to last, K1.

Repeat that row.

panel for TREE OF LIFE

17 stitch panel with a St. St. background

Row 1: K6, P2, K1, P2, K6 (RS).

P5, K2, P3, K2, P5 in row two.

K4, P2, (K1, P1) twice, K1, P2, K4 in the third row.

Row 4: P3, K2, P1, P1, P3, K2.

K2, P2, K1, P2, K3, P2, K1, P2, K2 in the fifth row.

Row 6: P1, K2, P1, P1, K2, (P1, K2) twice, P1.

Row 7: P2, K1, then P2 five times.

Row 8: K1, P1, K2, P3, K2, P1, K1, (P1, K2) twice.

Row 9: K1, P2, K1, P2, (K1, P2) twice, K1.

Row 10: P1, K1, 4 times (P1, K2), P1, K1, P1.

As in row 5, row 11.

P2, K1, P1, K2, (P1, K1) twice, P1, K2, P1, K1, P2, P2, K1, P1, P2. Row 12.

K3, (P2, K1) three times, P2, K3, row 13.

P3, K1, P1, K2, P3, K2, P1, K1, P3 in row 14.

As in row 3, row 15.

Row sixteen: P4, K1, twice (P1, K2), P1, K1, P4.

K5, P2, K3, P2, K5 on row 17.

Row 18: P5, K1, P5, (K1, P1) three times.

As in row 1, row 19.

P6, K1, P3, P6, P6 in row 20.

K7, P1, K1, P1, K7 in row 21.

P7, K1, P1, K1, P7 in row 22.

repeating these 22 rows

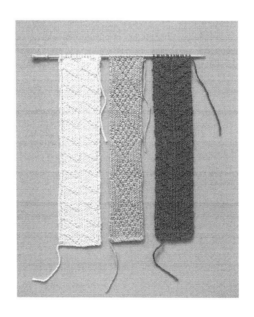

cable MOCK (left section of picture)

The diamond panel, double (middle section of picture)

Panel RIDGE AND FURROW (right area of picture)

Cable MOCK

7 stitches plus 2 multiples

Row 1 (RS): P3, K4, rep from last two stitches twice, P2.

Row 2: K2, P3, K2, continue to the final 2 stitches, K2.

P2, K1, P2, K2, repeat from the previous two stitches, P2. Row 3.

Row 4: K2, P1, K2, P2, repeat from the last two stitches, then K2.

P2, K3, P2, repeat from the last 2 stitches, P2, in row 5.

K3, P4, repeat from last 2 stitches, K2 in row 6.

P2, K5, repeat from the last stitch to the previous two, P2. Row 7.

K2, P5, repeat from the last two stitches to the end of the row, K2.

Repeat these 8 rows.

The diamond panel, double

13 stitch panel with a St. background

Row 1: K6, P1, K6 (RS).

P6, K1, P6 in row 2.

K5, P1, K1, P1, K5, third row.

Row 4: K1, P5, P5, P1.

Row 5: K4, P1, twice (K1, P1), K4.

Row 6: P4, K1, twice (P1, K1), P4.

Row 7: K3, P1, 3 repetitions of (K1, P1), K3.

Row 8: P3, K1, 3 repeats of (P1, K1), P3.

K2, P1, K1, P1, K3, P1, K1, P1, K2 in row 9.

P2, K1, P1, K1, P3, K1, P1, K1, P2 in row 10.

11th row: K5, (P1, K1, K1) twice, (K1, P1, K1) twice.

Row 12: P5, (K1, P1, P1) twice, K1, P1.

Row 13: As row 9, Row 14, Row 10, Row 15, Row 7, Row 8, Row 6, Row 17, Row 5, Row 18, Row 6, Row 19, Row 3, and Row 20, respectively.

20 rows of repetitions.

Panel RIDGE AND FURROW

15-st. multiples

Row 1 (RS): P1, K1, K1, P1, K5.

Row 2: P4, twice (K1, P2), K1, P4.

K3, (P1, K3) three times in row 3.

Row 4: P2, twice (K1, P4), K1, P2.

Row 5: P1, K5, K1, (P1, K5) twice.

Row 6: twice (K1, P6), K1.

Repetition: 6 rows.

THEATER panel (outer sections of picture)

Panel STEPS (inner areas of image)

ANCHOR design (central region of picture)

Panel with 11 stitches on a background of St.

(RS) K1, P1, K7, P1, K1, Rows 1 and 3

P1, K1, P7, K1, P1 in row two.

P1, K9, P1, on row 4.

Repeat these 4 rows.

Panel STEPS

5 stitches in a row on the background of St.

Row 1: P (RS)

Row 2: K1, P1, K1, twice.

Repeat those two rows.

11 stitch ANCHOR motif panel on a stitched backdrop

Row 1: K5, P1, K5, (RS)

Row 2: K1, P4, P4, P1.

Row 3: K3, twice (P1, K1), P1, K3.

P2, K1, P5, K1, P2 in Row 4.

Row 5: P1, K3, twice (P1, K1), K1.

K1, P9, K1 in row 6.

Row 7: twice (P1, K4), P1.

Row 8: P.

K5, P1, K5 in row 9.

Row 10: P.

K3, P5, K3 in row 11.

P3, K5, P3, Row 12.

Row 13: K.

P5, K1, P5, in row 14.

Row 15: K.

As in row 14 and row 16.

K4, P1, K1, P1, K4 on row 17.

(P3, K1) twice, P3 on row 18.

As in row 17 and row 19.

As row 14, row 20.

Row 21: K.

Row 22: P.

these 22 rows again.

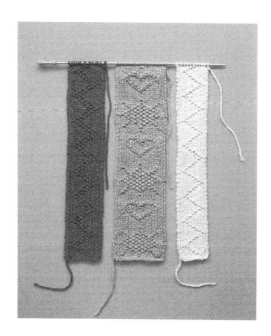

- Panel for marriage lines (left section of picture)
- Star and heart designs (middle section of image)
- LUMINARY panel (right area of picture)

Panel for marriage lines

13 stitch panel with a St. background

Row 1: P1, K1, twice, P1, K7, P1. (RS)

K1, P6, K1, P1, K1, P2, K1 in Row 2.

P1, K3, P1, K1, P1, K5, P1. Row 3.

K1, P4, K1, P1, K1, P4, in the fourth row.

P1, K5, P1, K1, P1, K3, P1. Row 5.

K1, P2, K1, P1, K1, P6, K1 in row 6.

Row 7: P1, K7, twice (P1, K1), P1.

As in row 6, row 8.

As in row 5, row 9.

As in row 4, row 10.

As in row 3, row 11.

As in row 2, row 12.

Do these 12 rows again.

Star and heart designs

19 stitch panel with a stitch backdrop

Row 1: K9, P1, K9 (RS).

Row 2: P.

Row 3: K3, twice (P1, K5), P1, K3.

Row 4: P4, K1, P3, K1, P1, K1, P3, K1, P4

Row 5: K5, (P1, K1) four times, P1, K5.

Row 6: P6, K1, P1, P1, (K1, P1) 3 times.

As row 5, row 7.

Row 8: P4, K1, P4, (K1, P1) 5 times.

Row 9: K1, P1, K1 nine times.

As in row 8, row 10.

As in row 7, row 11.

As in row 6, row 12.

As in row 5, row 13.

As in row 4, row 14.

As in row 3, row 15.

As in row 2, row 16.

As in row 1, row 17.

18 and 20 rows: P.

Row 19: K.

As in row 1, row 21.

P8, K3, P8 in row 22.

K7, P2, K1, P2, K7 on row 23.

P6, K2, P3, K2, P6 on row 24.

Row 25: twice (K5, P2), K5.

P4, K2, P7, K2, P4 in row 26.

K4, P2, K3, P1, K3, P2, K4 on row 27.

P4, K2, P2, K3, P2, K2, P4 in row 28.

K5, P4, K1, P4, K5 on row 29.

As row 24, row 30.

30 rows of repetitions.

LUMINARY panel

11 stitch panel with a St. background

Row 1: P1, K1, P1, K7, P1 (RS).

K1, P6, K1, P2, K1 in Row 2.

P1, K3, P1, K5, P1. Row 3.

K1, P4, K1, P4, K1 in row four.

P1, K5, P1, K3, P1 in Row 5.

K1, P2, K1, P6, K1 in row 6.

P1, K7, P1, K1, P1 in row 7.

As in row 6, row 8.

Row 9 is the same as rows 5, 10 and 11, 3 and 12, and Row 12.

Do these 12 rows again.

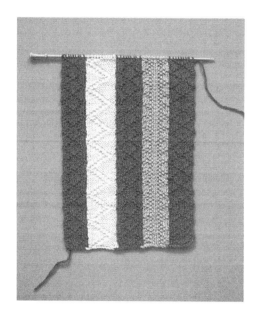

* DIAMOND panel, OPEN (outer and middle sections of picture)
* Panel ROUGH MARRIAGE LINES (left inner section of picture)
* Panel for SEEDED FLAGS (right inner section of picture)

The DIAMOND panel, OPEN

9 stitch panel with a St. St. background

Row 1: P1, K7, and P1 (RS).

P1, K1, P5, K1, P1 in Row 2.

K2, P1, K3, P1, K2 in row three.

P3, K1, P1, K1, P3 in row four.

K4, P1, K4 in row 5.

As in row 4, row 6.

As in row 3, row 7.

As in row 2, row 8.

Repeat these 8 rows.

Panel ROUGH MARRIAGE LINES

10 stitches in a row on a reverse stitch backdrop.

P7, K2, P8, K2, rep from first stitch to last, P1 (RS).

Row 2: From the start, P1, K1, P2, K6, repeat.

P5, K2, P1, K2, from the third row to the last.

P3, K1, P2, K4, repeat from the beginning for row 4.

P3, K2, P1, K4, from beginning to conclusion, row 5.

P5, K1, P2, K2, repeat till the end of row 6.

P1, K2, P1, K6, from beginning to conclusion, row 7.

As in row 6, row 8.

As in row 5, row 9.

As in row 4, row 10.

As in row 3, row 11.

As in row 2, row 12.

As in row 1, row 13.

P2, K8, rep through the end of row 14.

Repetition: 14 rows.

SEEDED FLAGS

panel 9 stitches on a background of St.

Row 1: K3, P1, K1, P1, K3, (RS)

P2, K1, P3, K1, P2 in row two.

Row 3: K1, P1, K1 four times.

Row 4: P1, (P1, K1, K1) twice, P1.

As in row 3, row 5.

As in row 2, row 6.

Repeat these 6 rows.

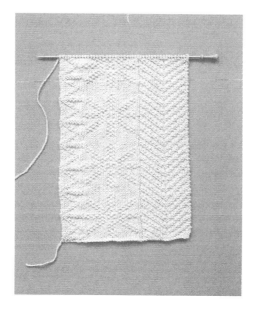

- Panel for FLAGS AND STRIPES (left section of picture)
- EASY STAR theme (middle section of image)
- DEFECTIVE CHEVRON panel (right section of picture)

STRIPES AND FLAGS panel

8 stitch panel with a St. St. background

Row 1: P (RS)

Row 2: K.

Row 3: P2, K1, K5, P2.

P2, K2, P4, Row 4.

K3, P2, K3 in row 5.

P4, K2, P2, P4, P6.

K1, P2, K5, in row 7.

Row 8: K2, P1, P5, P4.

: K2, P2, K4 Row 9

P3, K2, P3 on row 10.

K4, P2, K2 in row 11.

P1, K2, P5, row 12.

Do these 12 rows again.

PLAIN STAR motif

19 stitch panel with a stitch backdrop

Row 1: P (WS)

Row 2: K.

Row three: K1, P9, P9.

K8, P1, K1, P1, K8 in row 4.

Row 5: P1, K1, twice (P7, K1), P1.

K2, P1, K5, P1, K1, P1, K5, P1, Row 6:

Row 7: P5, K1, P5, (K1, P1) twice, (P1, K1).

Row 8: P1, K1, P1, K3, K2, (P1, K1, P1, K3) twice.

P3, K1, P1, (K1, P3) twice, K1, P1, K1, P3 in the ninth row.

Row ten: K4, P1, K1, K1 five times, K4.

Row 11: K1, P5, P5, (K1, P1) 4 times.

Row 12: K6, P1, K5, P1, K6.

Row 13: (P1, K1) 3 times, P2, K1, P1, K1, P2, (K1, P1) 3 times.

Row 14: (P1, K1) 3 times, P1, (K2, P1) twice, (K1, P1) 3 times.

Row 15: As row 13.

Row 16: As row 12. Row 17: As row 11. Row 18: As row 10.

Row 19: As row 9. Row 20: As row 8. Row 21: As row 7. Row 22: As row 6. Row 23: As row 5.

Row 24: As row 4.

Row 25: As row 3.

Row 26: As row 2.

Rep these 26 rows.

BROKEN CHEVRON panel

A panel of 18 sts on Reverse St st background

Row 1: (RS) (K1, P2, K2, P2, K1, P1) twice.

Row 2: K3, P2, K2, P2, K1, (P2, K2) twice.

Row 3: P1, K2, P2, K2, P3, (K2, P2) twice.

Row 4: K1, P2, K2, P2, K5, P2, K2, P2.

Repeat these 4 rows.

- Panel MOSS ZIGZAG (left section of picture)
- Panel with STOCKINETTE STITCH FLAGS (middle section of picture)
- Meeting with two herringbones (right area of view)

Panel MOSS ZIGZAG

14 stitch panel with a St. St. background

Row 1: (RS) twice (P1, K1, P1, K4)

Row 2: Twice (P4, K1, P1, K1).

((K1, P1) twice, K3, twice) Row 3.

(P3, (K1, P1) twice) twice in row 4.

K2, (P1, K1) twice, K3, (P1, K1) once, K1 in row five.

Row 6: P1, P2, (K1, P1) twice, P3, (K1, P1) once.

(K3, (P1, K1) twice) twice in row 7.

(P1, K1 twice, P3 twice) in row 8.

Row 9: K3, P1, K1, P1, (P1, K1) twice.

((K1, P1) twice, P3) twice in row 10.

As in row 7, row 11.

As in row 8, row 12.

As in row 5, row 13.

Rows 14, 6, and 15 are identical.

As in row 4, row 16.

Do these 16 rows again.

STOCKINETTE STITCH FLAGS panel

13 stitch flags on a reverse stitch background make up the.

Row 1: K4, P1, K3, P1, K4 (RS).

Row 2: (P3, K2, P3, twice)

Row 3: P3, K2, K2, P3, P3.

P1, K4, P3, K4, P1 in row four.

P5, K3, P5, P5, P5.

As with row 4, row 6, and row 3.

As in row 2, row 8.

Repeat these 8 rows.

Panel with Two Herringbones

17 stitch panel with a St. St. background

Row 1: (RS) twice (P1, K7), P1.

K1, P6, K1, P1, K1, P6, K1 in row two.

Row 3: P1, K5, P1, K5, (P1, K1) twice.

Row 4: K1, P4, 3 repetitions of K1, P1, K1, P4, K1.

P1, K3, (P1, K1) twice, K1, (K1, P1) twice, P1, K3.

Row 6: K1, P2, (P1, K1) twice, P3, (K1, P1, K1) once, P2, K1.

Row 7: K5, (P1, K1), (P1, K1) three times.

K2, P1, K1, P9, K1, P1, K2 on row eight.

Row 9: P1 twice, K9, P1 twice.

K2, P13, K2 in row 10.

P1, K15, P1 in row 11.

K1, P15, P1 in row 12.

Do these 12 rows again.

Ribs

Vertical lines on a relatively small scale characterize ribs, and this section presents a wide selection. To be truly practical for traditional welts, cuffs, and necklines, ribs should stretch, contract, and provide a firm, durable edging to the main fabric. However, some ribs perform these tasks more effectively

than others. The basic Knit One, Purl One and Knit Two, Purl Two ribs function the best of all. In contrast, for example, Blanket rib is not very elastic, and Raised Eyelet rib is not firm enough to do the same job. However, all have a place, and many fashionable garments look stunning with purely decorative welts or when ribs provide an overall pattern. Use needles one or two sizes smaller than those for the main fabric if you want to keep a welt firm and select a woolen yarn rather than a cotton for more elasticity.

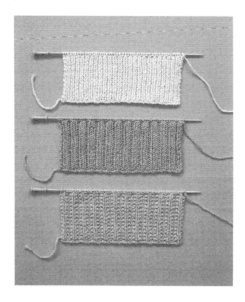

* PURL ONE rib, KNIT ONE rib (top section of picture)
* PURL TWO, KNIT TWO ribs (middle section of picture)
* SPRAYED rib (bottom area of view)

PURL ONE rib, KNIT ONE rib (reversible)

oddly sized stitches

Row 1: K1, P1, repeat from the first stitch to the last, K1.

P1, K1, repeat till the final stitch, P1; row 2.

Repeat those two rows.

PURL TWO, KNIT TWO ribs (reversible)

Numerous 4 stitches plus two

rows one: K2, P2, repeat from last two stitches, K2.

Row 2: K2, P2, P2, rep from previous two stitches.

Repeat those two rows.

SPRAYED rib (reversible)

Numerous 4 stitches plus three

K3, P1, K3, repeat from beginning to end.

K1, P1, K3, repeat from the last two stitches, P1, K1 in row two.

Repeat those two rows.

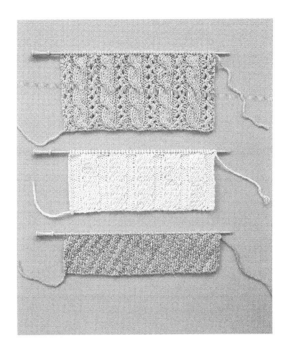

- Rib CABLE AND EYELET (top section of picture)
- RIB SPIRAL (middle section of the image)
- DIAGNOSTIC rib (bottom area of view)

Rib CABLE AND EYELET

10 st. multiples plus 4

Row 1 (RS): P2, K4, P2, K2tog, yarn, rep from the first stitch to last, P1.

Row 2 and all subsequent WS rows: K1, P2, K2, P4, K2, P2, rep from the first stitch to last, K1.

P1, yon, SKP, P2, C4F, P2, yarn, SKP, rep from the first stitch to last, P1. Row 3.

As in row 1, row 5.

P1, yon, SKP, P2, K4, P2, yarn, SKP, rep from the first stitch to last, P1. Row 7.

As in row 2, row 8.

Repeat these 8 rows.

RIB SPIRAL

9 stitches plus 3 multiples

Row 1 (RS): P3, C2B three times, rep from first to last three stitches, P3.

Row 2: K3, P6, repeat from last three stitches, K3.

Row three: P3, K1, C2B twice, K1, rep till the last three stitches, P3.

Row 4: K3, P6, repeat from last three stitches, K3.

Repeat these 4 rows.

DIAGNOSTIC Rib

4 st. multiples

Row 1 (RS): K2, P2, reps to completion.

Like row 1, row 2.

Row 3: K1, P2, K1, continue to the end.

P1, K2, P1, repeat in row 4 to the end.

P2, K2, rep through the end of row 5.

As in row 5, row 6.

P1, K2, P1, repeat from the beginning of row 7

Row 8: From the beginning, repeat K1, P2, and K1.

Repeat these 8 rows.

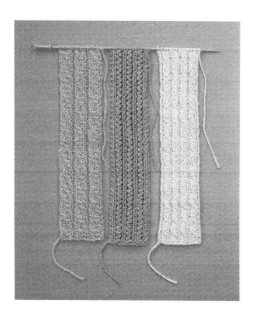

- BOUND rib (left section of picture)
- Rib RICKRACK (middle section of image)
- Rib twisted (right section of image)

BOUND rib

Multiples of 6 stitches Cr2F = K first stitch, then K second stitch, slipping both off LHN.

Row 1: P2, Cr2F, K2, rep from beginning to end (RS).

P4, K2, rep through on row 2 and all WS rows.

P2, K1, Cr2F, K1, repeat in row 3 to the finish.

P2, K2, Cr2F, repeat from beginning to end.

As in row 2, row 6.

Repetition: 6 rows.

Rib RICKRACK

Multiples of 5 stitches plus 1 Cr2F are K first stitch, K second stitch, then slip both off LHN.

Cr2PB = P first stitch and slide both off LHN after P second stitch on LHN tbl.

Row 1: From beginning to end, (RS) K1, P1, Cr2F, P1, K1.

P1, K1, Cr2PB, K1, repeat until the final stitch, P1. Row 2.

Repeat those two rows.

Rib twisted

Multiples of 4 stitches + 2 Cr2F equal K first stitch and slide both off LHN, then K second stitch on LHN TfL.

Rows 1 and 3: P2, K2, P2, rep from beginning to end (RS).

K2, P2, K2, repeat for row 2 and all WS rows.

P2, Cr2F, P2, rep from beginning to end.

As in row 2, row 6.

Repetition: 6 rows.

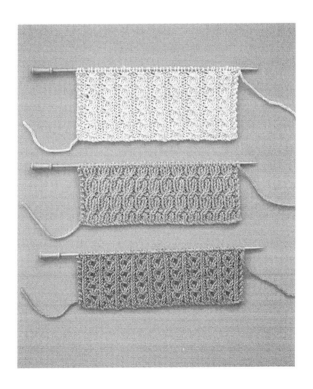

- RIB OF MOCK CABLE (top section of picture)
- BROKEN rib (middle section of picture)
- OPEN-TUNNELLED RIB (bottom section of picture)

RIB OF MOCK CABLE

Numerous 5 stitches plus two

P2, K3, repeat from last two stitches, P2, (RS): Row 1.

Row 2: K2, P3, K2, continue to the end.

P2, sl1, K2, yfrn, psso the K2 and yfrn, rep from the first two stitches to the final two, P2.

As in row 2, row 4.

Repeat these 4 rows.

Repeat these 4 rows.

BROKEN Rib

For multiples of 4 stitches plus 1 Cr3B, slip 2 stitches onto the CN, hold them at the back of the work, and then knit 1 stitch from the CN.

Row 1: P1, K1, rep from the first stitch to last, P1. (RS)

K1, P1, K1, repeat from the beginning of row 2 and all WS rows.

As in row 1, row 3.

P1, Cr3B, rep from the first stitch to last, P1. Row 5.

As in row 2, row 6.

Repetition: 6 rows.

OPEN-TUNNELLED RIB

5 stitches plus 3 multiples

Row 1 (RS): P1, K1 tbl, P1, K2, rep from first three stitches to final three, P1, K1 tbl, P1.

Row 2: From beginning to conclusion, K1, P1 tbl, K1, P2, K1, P1 tbl, K1, rep.

Row 3: P1, K1 tbl, P1, K1, yfwd, K1, rep from first three stitches till the last one, P1, K1 tbl, P1.

Row 4: From beginning to conclusion, K1, P1 tbl, K1, P3, K1, P1 tbl, K1, rep.

P1, K1 tbl, P1, K3, pass the third stitch on the right-hand needle over the first two stitches, repeat from to final three stitches, P1, K1 tbl, P1.

Repeat rows 2 through 5.

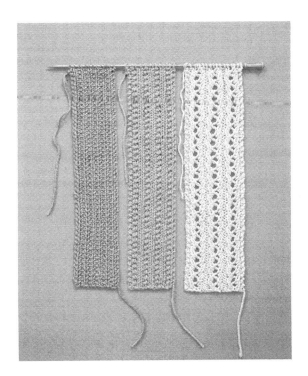

- Weaving rib (left section of picture)
- SPLIT rib (middle section of the image)
- RUBY rib (right area of view)

Weaving rib

two-stitch multiples plus one

(RS) K1, yfwd, sl1, ybk, rep from the first stitch to last, K1.

Replicate rows 1 and 2 in row 2.

SPLIT rib

Three-stitch multiples plus one

Row 1: (RS) K1, K1, but stop on LHN, yfwd, P1 into the same and next stitch together, ybk, rep from to the last stitch, K1.

Row 2: P.

Repeat those two rows.

RUBY rib

Numerous 5 stitches plus two

P2, K1, yfwd, SKP, P2, rep from beginning to end. Row 1. (RS)

Row 2: K2, P3, K2, continue to the end.

P2, K2tog, yfwd, K1, P2, rep every other row to the end.

As in row 2, row 4.

Repeat these 4 rows.

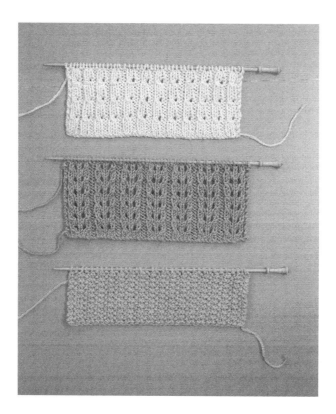

- BROADCAST rib (top section of picture)
- EYELET RISE RIB (middle section of picture)
- RIB BLANKET (bottom section of picture)

BROADCAST rib

Numerous 4 stitches plus two

Rows 1, 3, and 5: (WS) K2, P2, repeat from last 2 stitches to last stitch, K2.

P2, K2, P2, repeat rows 2 and 4 to the end.

P2, yrn, SKP, P2, rep from beginning to end. Row 6.

Repetition: 6 rows.

EYELET RISE RIB

7 stitches plus 2 multiples

(RS) P2, K2tog, yfwd, K1, yfwd, SKP, rep from first two stitches to last two, P2.

Row 2: From the beginning, repeat K2, P5, K2.

P2, K5, repeat from last two stitches to end of row, P2.

As in row 2, row 4.

Repeat these 4 rows.

RIB BLANKET

two-stitch multiples plus one

In Row 1, (RS) add 1 K to each stitch.

Row 2: From beginning to end, K2tog, P2tog, K2tog.

Repeat those two rows.

* RICKRACK DOUBLE RIB (top section of picture)
* CABLE ALTERNATING rib (middle section of image)
* RUBBER rib (bottom area of picture)

RICKRACK DOUBLE RIB

K 2nd st on LHN tbl, then K 1st st and slip both off LHN for multiples of 7 stitches plus 3 Cr2B.

Cr2F = K first stitch and slip both off LHN after K second stitch on LHN tfl.

Row 1: P3, Cr2B, Cr2F, repeat from last three stitches, P3 (RS).

Row 2: From the start, repeat K3, P4, K3.

P3, Cr2F, Cr2B, repeat from last three stitches, P3. Row 3.

Row 4: From the beginning, repeat K3, P4, K3.

Repeat these 4 rows.

CABLE ALTERNATING rib

77

9 stitches plus 3 multiples

Row 1: P3, K6, repeat from last 3 stitches, P3 (RS).

Row 2 and all WS rows: K3, P6, repeat from last stitch to third stitch, K3.

P3, C4B, K2, repeat from last stitch to third row, P3.

Row 5: P3, K2, C4F, rep from first 3 stitches to last 3, P3.

As in row 2, row 6.

Recite rows 3-6.

RUBBER rib

Numerous 5 stitches plus two

P2, yfrn, K2tog, tbl, K1, P2, rep from beginning to end.

Row 2: K2tog tbl, P1 tbl, K2tog tbl, K2, rep from beginning to end.

Repeat those two rows.

4.3 Textured stitches

This section draws together stitch patterns that create a textured fabric— some of them subtly and others more flamboyantly. They also have a mixed heritage. Trinity stitch is often associated with Aran designs and has distinctly religious connotations with its three-in-one and one-in-three construction. The name Linen stitch reflects the fabric it creates, and Gathered stitch delivers just what it promises.

The stitch patterns represent a real exploration of various techniques to create different textures. Twisting knit stitches across a purl background takes them on a winding path to the left or right. Crossing two knit stitches produce a miniature cable, which can be worked either with or without a cable needle according to preference. Both of these techniques reduce the elasticity of the fabric, as with the Double Trellis pattern. Very firm fabrics evolve from stitches such as Risotto and Spine stitch. Other methods include matching increases and decreases to make textures, such as Trinity stitch and wrapping the yarn around stitches to cluster them or the needle to elongate them.

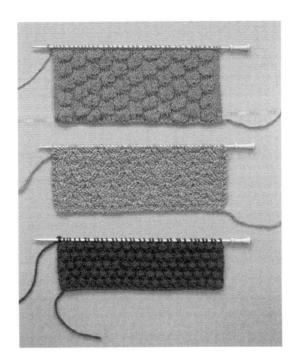

- STITCH LONG BOBBLE (top section of picture)
- TRELLIS style (middle section of image)
- Cherry stitch (bottom section of image)

STITCH LONG BOBBLE

6 stitches plus 3 multiples

Row 1: P to the end (WS).

Row 2: K1, K3, (K1, yfwd, K1, into next stitch, K1, (turn, P5, turn, K5, twice, K1, (turn, P5, turn, K5)

rep until the final 2 stitches, then knit 2.

Row 3: P1, P2, P2tog, P1, P2tog tbl, P1, rep from first two stitches, P2, repeat.

K3, K4, (K1, yfwd, K1) into the next stitch, K1, (turn, P5, turn, K5) twice, K3, K4, (turn, P5, turn, K5)

K6 from the last 6 stitches.

P3, P3, P2tog, P1, P2tog tbl, rep from first 6 stitches to last 6, P6.

Repeat rows 2 through 5.

TRELLIS style

8-st increments plus 2

Cr2B = K first stitch and slip both off LHN after K second stitch on LHN tbl.

Cr2F = K first stitch and slip both off LHN after K second stitch on LHN TfL.

(WS) P4, K2, P6, K2, repeat from last 4 stitches, P4; row 1

Row 2: Repeat K2, Cr2B, P2, Cr2F, and K2 from the beginning.

P3, K4, P4, K4, repeat the previous three stitches, P3. Row 3.

Row 4: K1, P4, Cr2F, repeat from the first stitch to the last, K1.

K2, P6, K2, repeat from the beginning of row 5

Row 6: From the beginning, repeat P2, Cr2F, K2, Cr2B, and P2.

Row 7: K3, P4, K4, P4, repeat from the third stitch onward, K3.

P3, Cr2F, Cr2B, P4, Cr2F, Cr2B, rep from last three stitches, P3. Row 8.

Repeat these 8 rows.

Cherry stitch

two-stitch multiples plus one

1st row: (RS) K.

Row 2: K1, rep from beginning to end (P1, yarn, P1, yarn, P1) into the next stitch.

Row 3: P.

Row 4: From beginning to end, K1, yfwd, sl2, P3tog, p2sso, and K1 must be used.

Row 5: K.

Row 6: K1, K1, (P1, yarn, P1, yarn, P1) into the following stitch, rep from to the final two stitches, K2.

Row 7: P.

Row 8: K1, K1, yfwd, sl2, P3tog, p2sso, ybk, rep from first two stitches to the last two, K2.

Repeat these 8 rows.

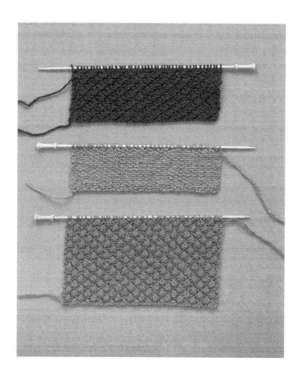

- Stitched in SLIPPED GRANITE (top section of picture)
- Cloth stitch (middle section of the image)
- STITCH TRINITY (bottom area of view)

Stitched in SLIPPED GRANITE

Numerous 4 stitches plus two

Row 1: (WS) K1, P1, rep through the finish line.

P1, ybk, sl1, K2, yfrn, psso the K2 and yfrn, rep from the last two stitches, P1, row 2

K1.

As in row 1, row 3.

Row 4: From beginning to conclusion, perform P1, K1, P1, ybk, sl1, K2, yarn, and psso the K2 and yfrn.

Repeat these 4 rows.

Cloth stitch

2 st. multiples

Row 1: (RS) K1, YFWD, SL1, YBK, rep all the way through.

P1, YBK, Sl1, YFWD, rep from beginning to end.

Repeat those two rows.

STITCH TRINITY

Numerous 4 stitches plus two

Row 1: P (RS)

Row 2: K1, (P1, K1, K1) into the next stitch, P3tog, rep from there until the last stitch, K1.

Row 3: P.

Row 4: K1, P3tog, (K1, P1, K1) into the following stitch, rep from to the last stitch, K1.

Repeat these 4 rows.

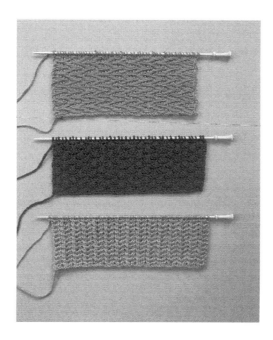

- Brocade woven (top section of picture)
- BLUESTONE stitch (middle section of image)
- the SPINE stitch (bottom section of image)

Brocade woven

10 stitch multiples plus 2

Row 1 (RS): K2, yfwd, sl3, ybk, K1, rep from the first stitch to last, K1.

Row 2: P2, rep from the first stitch to last, sl1, ybk, sl3, yfwd.

Row 3: K2, yfwd, sl3, rep from first to last five stitches, ybk, K2, yfwd, sl2, ybk, K1.

Row 4: P2, ybk, sl3, yfwd, rep from first five stitches to the final one, sl1, ybk, sl2, yfwd, sl1.

Row 5: K2, rep from the first stitch to last, K1, yfwd, sl3, ybk, K2.

Row 6: sl1, P1, yfwd, sl3, P1, rep from the first stitch to last, sl1.

As row 5, row 7.

As in row 4, row 8.

As in row 3, row 9.

As in row 2, row 10.

Ten rows of repetitions.

BLUESTONE stitch

4 st. multiples

Row 1 (RS): K1, yfwd, K1, next stitch, P3, repeat from beginning to end.

P3tog, K3, rep through the end of row 2.

P3, (K1, yfwd, K1) into the following stitch, rep from beginning to end.

K3, P3tog, repeat from the beginning of row 4

Repeat these 4 rows.

SPINE stitch

Multiples of 4 stitches

Cr2B = K first stitch and slip both off LHN after K second stitch on LHN tbl.

Cr2F = K first stitch and slip both off LHN after K second stitch on LHN TfL.

Row 1: Cr2B and Cr2F from beginning to end (RS).

Row 2: P.

Repeat those two rows.

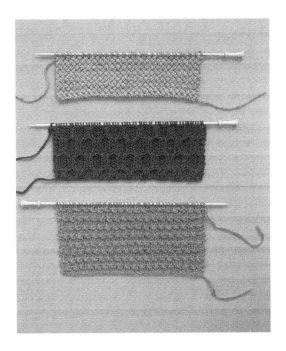

* STITCHED PLAITED BASKET (top section of picture)
* The TRELLIS stitch (middle section of the image)
* PINK stitch (bottom area of image)

STITCHED PLAITED BASKET

2 st. multiples

Cr2B = K first stitch and slip both off LHN after K second stitch on LHN tbl.

Cr2F = P first stitch on LHN, then P second stitch on LHN, and slip both off LHN.

Row 1: Cr2B from beginning to end (RS).

P1, Cr2F, repeat from the first stitch to last, P1.

Repeat those two rows.

Repeat those two rows.

The TRELLIS stitch

6 st. multiples

T3L = place first on CN and hold it in front of the work, P2, and K1 from CN

T3R = K1, P2 from CN while holding 2 stitches on the CN at the back of the work.

Rows 1 and 3: P2, K2, P2, rep from beginning to end (RS).

Rows 2 and 4 are K2, P2, K2, repeat.

T3R, T3L from beginning to conclusion, row 5.

P1, K4, P1, rep from the beginning for Rows 6, 8, and 10.

Rows 7 and 9: From the beginning, repeat K1, P4, and K1.

Row 11: T3L, T3R, rep all the way through.

Like row 2, row 12

Do these 12 rows again.

PEBBLE stitch

Multiples of 2 stitches

1st row: (RS) K.

Row 2: P.

Row 3: K1, K2, rep from the first stitch to last, K1.

Row 4: K1, rep from the first stitch to the last stitch, K1, K1 in a horizontal bar before the next stitch.

Repeat these 4 rows.

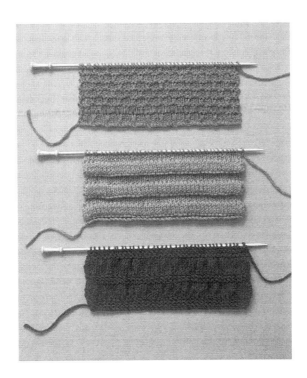

- SLICING RIDGED stitch (top section of picture)
- STOCKINETTE TUCKED stitch (middle section of picture)
- COLLECTED stitch (bottom area of the image)

SLICING RIDGED stitch

4 st. multiples

Row 1: (RS) K3, sl1, rep all the way through.

Row 2: ybk, sl1, yfwd, P3, rep through the last rep.

As in row 1, row 3.

Row 4: K.

K1, sl1, ybk, K2, rep from beginning to end. Row 5.

P2, sl1, yfwd, P1, rep from beginning to conclusion.

As row 5, row 7.

Row 8: K.

Repeat these 8 rows.

STOCKINETTE TUCKED stitch

any number's multiples

1, 3, and 5th rows: (RS) Rows 2, 4, 6, and 7 are K. Rows 8 through 12 are P. Rows 9 through 11 are K.

Fold at the ridge in row 13, pick up the first stitch of row 2 from the back, join it to the first stitch on the LHN tbl, and repeat from there.

P for rows 14, 16, and 18, and K for rows 15, 17, and 19.

Rows 2 through 19 should be repeated.

GATHERED stitch

Rows 1-6: K.

In Row 7, (RS) add 1 K to each stitch.

P for rows 8, 10, and 12. K for rows 9 and 11.

K2tog, repeat from beginning to end.

Rows 2 through 13 should be repeated.

* Stitch in RISOTTO (top section of picture)
* FLUFF stitch (middle section of picture)
* STITCH CLAM (bottom area of picture)

Stitch in RISOTTO (reversible)

2 st. multiples

(RS) K in Rows 1 and 3.

Row 2: P2tog, leaving the last two stitches on LHN, you, then K tog, repeat from beginning to end.

P1, P2tog, ybk, K tog same 2 sts, rep from the first stitch to last, P1. Row 4:

Row 5: K.

Repeat rows 2 through 5.

FLUFF stitch

2 st. multiples

1st row: (RS) K.

Row 2: K.

Row 3: K1, K1, from beginning to end, rep through the center of stitch in the row below.

Row 4: K1, repeat from beginning to end, k tog next stitch and longer loop at its base.

K1, rep from beginning to end, K1 through the center of stitch in row below, row 5.

Row 6: K1, K to the following stitch and the larger loop at its base, and repeat from there.

Recite rows 3-6.

CLAM stitch

Multiples of 6 sts plus 1

1st row: (RS) K.

P1, (yarn, P1) five times, P1, rep till the end of row two.

Row 3: K1, sl5 to RHN dropping extra loops, pass 5 sts back to LHN, (yfrn, K1, (yfrn, P1, yo, K1) twice) into same 5 sts tog, rep from to last st, K1.

Row 4: P1, K5, removing superfluous loops, rep from the first stitch to the last, P1.

Row 5: K.

Row 6: P4, (yarn, P1) 5 times, P1, rep from to last 3 sts, P3.

Row 7: K3, K1, knit next 5 stitches as in row 3, rep from there until the final 4 stitches, K4.

Row 8: P4, K5 dropping extra loops, P1, rep from to last 3 sts, P3.

Repeat these 8 rows.

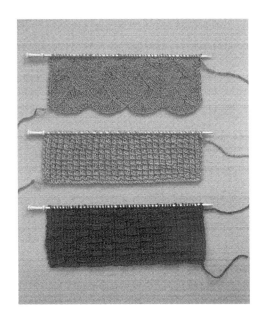

- the pattern of OVERLAPPING LEAVES (top section of picture)
- BOOM stitch (middle section of the image)
- STITCH: WOVEN LADDER (bottom area of view)

OVERLAPPING LEAVES

24 stitch multiples plus one

K1, M1, SKP, K4, K2tog, K3, M1, K1, M1, SKP, K4, K2tog, Row 1 (RS)

M1, K1, repeat until done.

P on row 2 and every WS row.

Row 3: K1, M1, K1, SKP, K2, K2tog, K2, K2tog, K4, M1, K1, M1, K4, SKP,

K1, M1, K1, repeat until the end.

K1, M1, K2, SKP, K2tog, K5, M1, K1, M1, K5, SKP, K2tog, K2, M1, K1, M1, Row 5

From beginning to end, K1.

Row 7: K1, M1, SKP, K4, K2tog, M1, K1, M1, SKP, K3, M1,

From beginning to end, K1.

Row 9: K1, M1, K4, SKP, K2, K2tog, K1, SKP, K2, K2tog, K4, (K1, M1) twice.

M1, K1, repeat until done.

K1, M1, K2, SKP, K2tog, K2, M1, K1, M1, K5, M1, Row 11

From beginning to end, K1.

Row 12: P.

Do these 12 rows again.

BOOM stitch

2 st. multiples

Row 1 (RS): K1, yarn, K2, previous yarn passed over K2, rep from to the last stitch, K1.

Row 2: P.

Repeat those two rows.

STITCH: WOVEN LADDER

8-stitch multiples plus one

Row 1: K5, YFWD, SL3, YBK, rep from the first stitch to last, K1 (RS).

P1, ybk, sl3, yfwd, P5, rep from beginning to end. Row 2.

As in row 1, row 3.

Row 4: P.

K1, yfwd, sl3, ybk, K5, rep from beginning to end. Row 5.

P1, P4, ybk, sl3, yfwd, P1, rep from beginning to end for row six.

As row 5, row 7.

As in row 4, row 8.

Repeat these

Stich in RIPPLE

3 st. multiples

Row 1 (RS): K2tog, but leave on LHN; K first stitch again; slide both off LHN;

from beginning to end, K1.

Row 2: P.

K1, K2tog, K into the first stitch one more as row 1, repeat from beginning to end.

Row 4: P.

Repeat these 4 rows.

TRELLIS DOUBLE pattern

6 stitches plus 4 multiples

RT2R = (raised twist right) K 1st and 2nd sts tog TBL RT2L = (presented twist left)

(augmented twist right) K2tog, leaving stitches on the left-hand needle, K first stitch again and slip both from LHN

P for row one and all WS rows.

Row 2: RT2L, RT2R twice; repeat from first 4 stitches to last 4, RT2L, RT2R.

Row 4: K1, RT2R, RT2L, twice; rep from the first stitch to last, K1.

Row 6: K2, RT2L twice, rep from beginning to end.

Row 8: K1, RT2R, rep from first three stitches to final two, RT2L, K1.

RT2R, RT2L, RT2R twice, rep from the last 2 stitches, RT2L, row 10.

K3, RT2R twice, K2, rep through the last stitch, K1, for row 12.

Do these 12 rows again.

STRIPE stitch

8 st. multiples plus 4

Slip 6 stitches onto the RHN, dropping any extra loops. Slip the same 6 stitches onto the LHN.

K the first, second, and third stitches, then slip all six stitches off the needle in one motion.

Cr6R = slip 6 stitches onto RHN, dropping extra loops, slip same 6 stitches onto LHN, K.

K the first, second, and third stitches, then slip all six stitches off the needle in a row.

1: (RS) K.

Row 2: K3, yfrn, P1, (yarn, P1) five times, K2, repeat from the third stitch to the end, K1.

K1, K2, Cr6R, repeat from the third stitch to last, K3.

Row 4: K1, P2, K2, yfrn, P1, (yarn, P1) five times, K2, rep from first five stitches to the final five, P4.

K1.

K5, K2, Cr6L, rep from last 5 stitches, K7 for row 5.

Repeat rows 2 through 5.

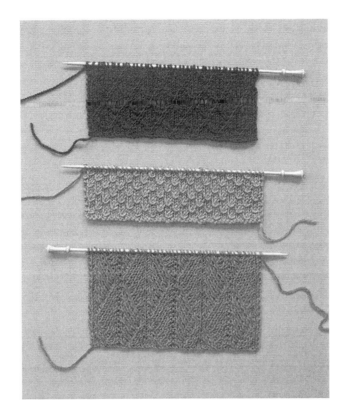

- TRELLIS design in DIAMOND (top section of picture)
- GRAIN DIAGONAL stitch (middle section of the image)
- The pattern of INTERLOCKING LEAVES (bottom section of picture)

TRELLIS design in DIAMOND

6 stitches plus 2 multiples

Cr2B = K first stitch and slip both off LHN after K second stitch on LHN tbl.

Cr2F = K first stitch and slip both off LHN after K second stitch on LHN TfL.

(RS) K3, Cr2B, K4, rep from the first stitch to the last five stitches, K3, Cr2B.

P on row 2 and every WS row.

K2, Cr2B, Cr2F, rep from last two stitches, K2, in row three.

K1, Cr2B, K2, Cr2F, from the first stitch to last, K1. Row 5.

Cr2B, K4, repeat from previous 2 stitches, Cr2B, as Row 7.

K1, Cr2F, K2, Cr2B, from the first stitch to last, K1. Row 9.

K2, Cr2F, Cr2B, repeat from last 2 stitches, K2, end of row 11.

Row 12: P.

Do these 12 rows again.

GRAIN DIAGONAL stitch

A multiple of 4 stitches + 1

(RS) K in Rows 1 and 3.

P1, yarn, P2, pass thread over P2, P2, rep from beginning to end in row two.

P1, P2, yarn, P2, pass thread over P2, rep from beginning to end in row 4.

Repeat these 4 rows.

The pattern of INTERLOCKING LEAVES

16-stitch multiples plus one

Cr2B = K first stitch and slip both off LHN after K second stitch on LHN tbl.

Cr2F = K first stitch and slip both off LHN after K double stitch on LHN TfL.

Row 1 (RS): K1, K1, P1, Cr2B, Cr2F, twice, Cr2F, K2, rep from

the end.

P on row 2 and every WS row.

Row 3: K1, P1, K1, Cr2B, Cr2F twice, K1, Cr2F, K1, rep from to

end.

Row 5: P1, Cr2B twice, Cr2F once, K2, K1, Cr2B twice, Cr2F once, rep from beginning to end.

Row 7: K1, P1, K1, Cr2B, Cr2F twice, K1, Cr2F once, K1, rep from to

end.

Row 9: P1, Cr2B 3 times, K2, K1, Cr2F 3 times, rep from beginning to end.

Row 11: K1, P1, K1, Cr2F three times, K1, Cr2B three times, K1, and repeat from there.

Like row 9 and row 13.

As in row 7, row 15.

As in row 5, row 17.

As in row 3, row 19.

As in row 1, row 21.

Row 23: K1, Cr2B, 3 K1, P1, K1, Cr2F, 3 K1, rep from beginning to end.

Row 25: P1, Cr2F 3 times, K2, K1, Cr2B 3 times, rep from beginning to end.

As row 23, row 27.

Row 28: P.

Repetition: 28 rows.

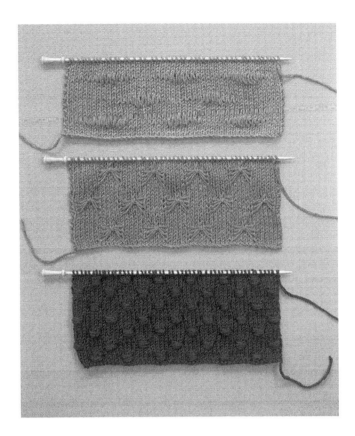

- A LONG stitch (top section of picture)
- Butterfly Woven Stitch (middle section of picture)
- CUSHION stitch (bottom area of image)

A LONG stitch

fourteen stitches plus five

Row 1 and Row 3: (RS) K.

P. Rows 2 and 4:

Row 5: K4, (K1, yfrn) 3 times, 4 times, (K1, yfrn twice), 3 times, K4, rep from the first stitch to final stitch, K1.

P on row 6, removing any unnecessary loops.

K in rows 7 and 9.

P. Rows 8 and 10:

Row 11: K7, K4, (K1, yfrn) three times, (K1, yfrn twice), four times, (K1, yfrn) three times; rep from the first stitch to last, K12;

Row 12: P, removing any more loops.

Do these 12 rows again.

Butterfly Woven Stitch

Slip RHN under 4 long loops, knit the next stitch, and draw the next stitch under the long loops to form a butterfly with multiples of 10 stitches plus 7. Rows 1, 3, 5, and 7: (RS) K6, yfwd, sl5, ybk, K5, rep from the last stitch to the beginning, K1.

All WS rows except row 2: P. Row 9: K8, make a butterfly, K9, rep from the eighth stitch to the ninth, make a butterfly, K8.

K1, yfwd, sl5, ybk, K5, yfwd, sl5, ybk, rep from first to final stitch, K1. Rows 11, 13, 15, and 17.

Row 19: K3, butterfly; K9, butterfly; rep from first three stitches to last three; K3.

P. Repeat these 20 rows.

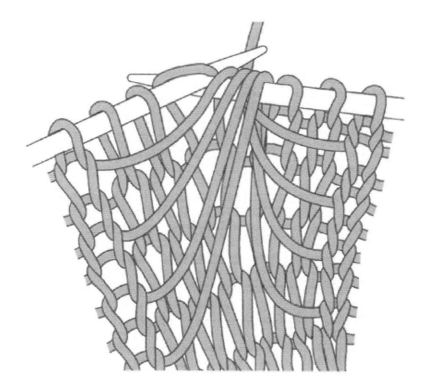

Multiples of 8 stitches plus 5 make a cluster by slipping the following three stitches onto the center needle, wrapping the yarn around the stitches six times in the opposite direction, and then knitting three stitches from the center needle.

1st row: (RS) K.

All WS rows except row 2: P.

Row 3: K5, form a cluster, rep till the final 5 stitches, K5.

As in row 3, row 5.

Row 7: K4, from the first stitch to the final five stitches, K1, make a cluster.

Row 8: P.

Repeat these 8 rows.

4.4 Edgings

Most stitch patterns require an edge, also known as ribbing, to prevent the knitted fabric from curling or to give the finished item greater strength. Some edgings are incorporated horizontally to create a band that, when gently stretched, is long enough to meet the edge and be sewed around it. Before or after knitting the main fabric, other pieces might be incorporated as a unit. It's a good idea to knit a gauge swatch because the length of the knitted-on version relies on the gauge and the number of stitches.

This collection of edgings includes more dramatic Double Frill, Ruffled, and Knotted edgings in addition to the extremely straightforward finishes shown opposite. It has some lovely open boundaries. All of these may be knitted with medium-weight yarns to give them a robust feel, and some look lovely with extremely fine Shetland wool to provide them with the gossamer-like quality of Shetland lace. You can get inspiration from the pictures, but try different things for varied results.

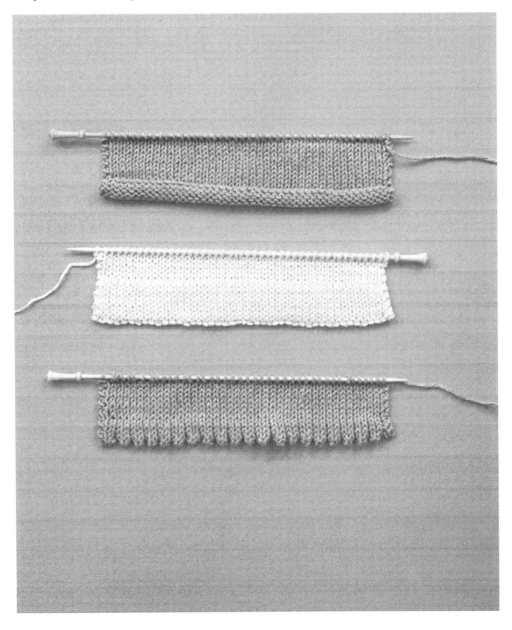

- Edged with STOCKINETTE STITCH (top section of picture)

- HE PURL RIDGE (middle area of view)
- Hem PICOT RIDGE (bottom area of view)

Edged With Stockinette Stitch

Required: Cast on stitches for finished number

(RS) K for Rows 1, 3, and 5. Rows 2, 4, and 6: hem P. PURL RIDGE

Required: Cast on stitches for finished number

1, 3, 5, and 7th rows: (RS) Rows 2, 4, 6, and 8 in K. P. Row 9: Rows 10, 12, 14, 16, and 18 are worked in P. Rows 11, 13, and 15 are worked in K. Fold under the purl ridge and slip stitch the edge in place.

Hem Picot Ridge

two-stitch multiples plus one

Row 1 and 3: (RS) Row 2, as well as all WS rows: K1, yfwd, K2tog, rep from beginning to end. P. Row 5.

Rows 7, 8, and 9: K. Slip stitches the edging along the picot row by folding the row under.

- EDGING WITH SIMPLE LOOP (top section of picture)
- Edging TREE OF LIFE (middle section of image)
- A WAVE's edge (bottom area of picture)

EDGING WITH A SIMPLE LOOP

6 stitches plus 3 multiples (top edge decreases to half as many sts)

(RS) K3, bind off 3 stitches, K3, rep from beginning to end.

Rows 2-5: K.

Edging TREE OF LIFE

Numerous 13-st stitches

Row 1: From beginning to conclusion, K1, yfwd, K4, SK2P, K4, and K1 (RS).

Row 2: From starting to close, P2, K9, P2.

Row 3: From beginning to conclusion, K2, yfwd, K3, SK2P, K3, yfwd, K2, rep.

P3, K7, P3, repeat from beginning to end.

Row 5: From beginning to conclusion, K3, yfwd, K2, SK2P, K2, yfwd, K3, rep.

P4, K5, P4, repeat from the beginning of row 6

Row 7: From beginning to conclusion, K4, yfwd, K1, SK2P, K1, yfwd, K4, rep.

Row 8: P5, K3, P5, continue to the end.

Rep from beginning to finish of Row 9: K5, yfwd, SK2P, K5, yfwd.

Edging in row 10: P. WAVE

18 stitch multiples plus 2

1st row: (RS) K.

Row 2: P.

Row 3: K1, K2tog three times, K2tog three times, (yfwd, K1) six times, rep from to the last stitch, K1.

Row 4: K. Rows 5–12: Repetition of rows 1-4.

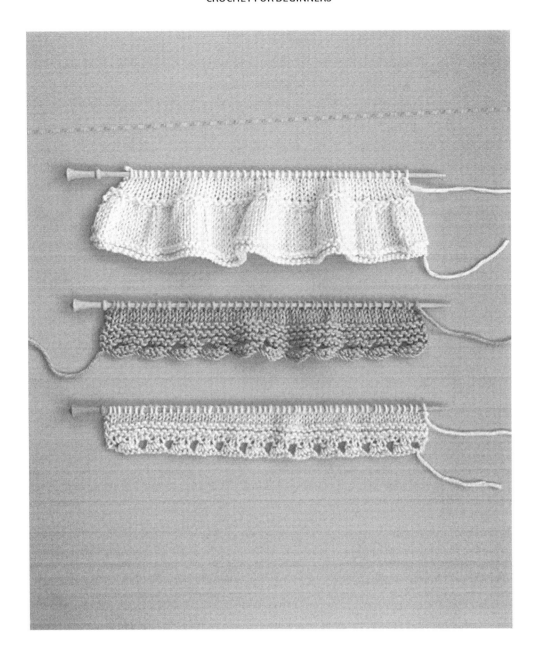

- Frill in GARTER STITCH (top section of picture)
- A TIN LOOP border (middle section of the image)
- SMALL LACE trim (bottom area of view)

Frill in GARTER STITCH

Half the required number of stitches should be cast on.

Rows 1-3: K.

(RS) P for Rows 4, 6, 8, and 10.

5, 7, 9, and 11th rows: K.

K2tog to end of row 12.

A TIN LOOP border.

6 stitches plus 2 multiples (top edge decreases to two-thirds as many sts)

Row 1: (RS) K2, bind off 4 stitches, leaving the final stitch on the right-hand needle, K1, repeat from there.

K2, yfrn, K2, rep from beginning to end.

Row 3: K2, rep from beginning to end, inc 1 K in yarn.

Rows 4-7: K.

SMALL LACE trim

Multiples of 5 stitches plus 2 (top edge drops to 4 stitches for each multiple, plus 5 rather than 2) Row 1: (RS) K1, yfwd, K5, rep from to last st, K1, lift the second, third, fourth, and fifth stitches over the first stitch and off the left-hand needle.

Row 2: P1, yon, K1 tbl into next stitch, K1, P1, rep from beginning to end.

Row 3: K2, K1 tbl, K3, K1 tbl, rep from the first stitch to the last two stitches, K2.

Rows 4-6: K.

a KNOTTED edge (top section of picture)

A RUFFLED edge (middle section of the image)

A LONG LOOP border (bottom area of view)

KNOTTED edge

sts in multiples of 12

Step 1: Cast on 6 stitches and knit 20 rows in St ink, beginning with a K row. Cut yarn, leaving stitches on a holder. Create one more strip.

Step 2: Create whichever many sets of two strips are necessary.

Step 3 is to place all strips with RS facing on LHN. Put the first strip across the second strip. Twist the cast-on edge of the second strip so that RS still faces forward and bring it in front of the first strip. Tuck it in between the two strips. Place the cast-on edge below the first strip's stitches. Toggle each stitch on the first strip with a loop from the cast-on edge of the second strip.

Step 4: Knit the second strip together by twisting the remaining cast-on edge behind the stitches.

Repeat step 5 to form rem knots. Knit

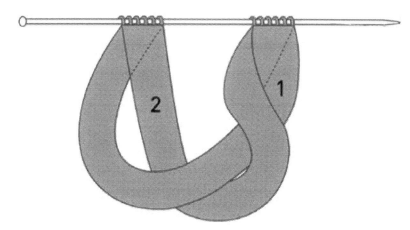

Knit the top edge of strip 1 to the bind-off edge of strip 2, as well as the top border of strip 2.

A RUFFLED edge

Multiple 16 stitches plus 5 (top edge drops to 6 stitches with each additional stitch) Row 1: K5, P11, K5, rep from beginning to end (WS).

2nd row: P5, K2tog, K7, SKP, P5, repeat from beginning to end.

R3: K5, P9, K5, repeat from beginning to end.

P5, K2tog, K5, SKP, P5, from beginning to end. Row 4.

K5, P7, K5, repeat from beginning to end.

P5, K2tog, K3, SKP, P5, repeat from beginning to end.

K5, P5, K5, repeat from beginning to end.

P5, K2tog, K1, SKP, P5, repeat from beginning to end for row 8.

Row 9: K5, P3, K5, continue to the end.

P5, SK2P, P5, from beginning to conclusion, row 10.

K5, P1, K5, repeat from the beginning of row 11

A LONG LOOP borders

Multiples of 11 stitches plus 2 (top edge drops to 6 stitches with each additional stitch) Row 1: P (RS)

Row 2: K2, K1, slip the last stitch back onto LHN, raise the following eight stitches over it and off LHN, yarn twice, K into slip stitch on LHN once more, K2, rep from beginning to end.

Row 3: K1, P2tog, slip one of the additional loops off LHN (K1, K1 TBL) thrice into the remaining loop, P1, rep from the last stitch to first, K1.

Rows 4-8: K.

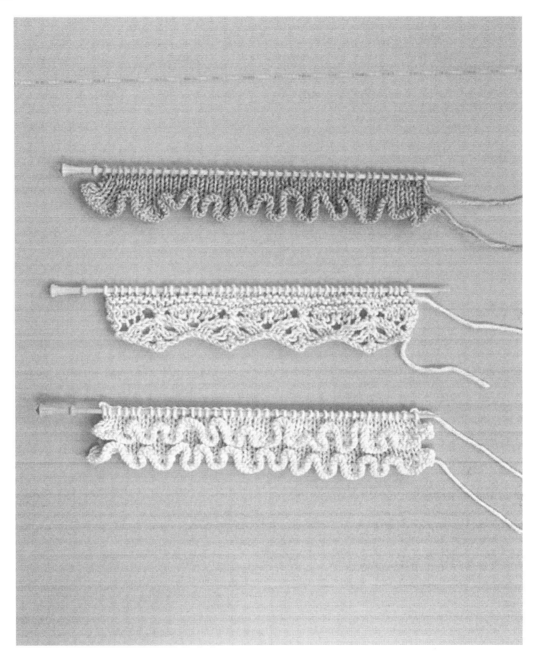

- ONLY one frill (top section of picture)
- A SCALLOP's edge (middle section of image)
- TWO ruffles (bottom area of picture)

ONLY one frill

Cast on four times the necessary stitches to complete one row.

Row 1: (RS) K2, cross the second stitch over the first and of the right hip.

P2tog, repeat from beginning to end.

A SCALLOP's edge

Multiples of 13 stitches plus 2 (top edge drops to 12 stitches for each multiple, plus 3 rather than 2). K1, K2, SKP, sl2, K3tog, p2sso, K2tog, K2, rep from the first stitch to last, K1 (RS).

Row 2: P4, turn, P1, yarn, P6, rep from first five stitches to last four, yarn, P1, yarn, P4.

Row 3: K2, SKP, K1, K2tog, K2, yfwd, rep from the first stitch to last, K1, yfwd.

Row 4: P1, P2, yarn, yarn, P3, yarn, yarn, rep from the first stitch to the last stitch, P1.

K2, yfwd, K1, yfwd, SKP, K1, SK2P, K1, K2tog, (yfwd, K1) twice, rep from the first stitch to last, K1 in row five.

Row 6: P.

Row 7: K5, yfwd, sl2, K3, p2sso, yfwd, K7; rep from last 10 stitches to the beginning, yfwd, sl2, K3, p2sso, yfwd, K5.

Rows 8-10: K.

TWO frills

Cast on four times the necessary stitches to complete one row. It takes three knitting needles. Work a single frill (see stitch pattern at left), then 2 rows of st. St., and leave on the extra needle in step 1. Place the same number of stitches and move on to Step 2:

Row 1: (RS) K2, cross the second stitch over the first and of the right hip.

P2tog, repeat from beginning to end.

3, 5, 7, and 9th rows: K.

4, 6, 8, and 10th rows: P.

Step 3: Layer the Single frill over the Double ruffle while keeping the stitches on the needles. On both needles, knit the first stitch together. Repeat, knitting the final row of both groups of sts together.

- A FEATHER edge (top section of picture)
- A BEADED border (middle section of the image)
- A FERN edge (bottom area of view)

A FEATHER edges

Add 9 stitches.

Row 1 (RS): sl1, K1, yfwd, K2tog, K1, yfwd, K2

2, 4, 6, and 8th rows: K.

sl1, K1, yfwd, K2tog, K2, yfwd, K2tog, K2, in row three.

Row 5: K1, sl1, yfwd, K2tog, K3, K2, yfwd, K2.

Row 7: sl1, K1, yfwd, K2tog, K1, yfwd, K2tog, K2, yfwd.

Row 9: K1, sl1, yfwd, K2tog, K2, K2, yfwd, K2tog, K5,

Row 10: K to finish and bind off 4 stitches. Follow these ten rows again.

A BEADED border

Add 8 stitches.

Row 1: Sl1, K1, Yarn, P2tog, (K1, P1, K1) into next st, rep from once in reverse (RS).

(K3, yarn, P2tog) twice, K2, row 2.

Sl1, K1, (string, P2tog, K3) twice in row 3.

Row 4: Bind off 2 stitches, yarn, P2tog; then bind off the following 2 stitches, yarn, P2tog, K2.

Repeat these 4 rows.

A FERN edges

Add 10 stitches.

Row 1: (RS) sl1, K2, yfwd, K2tog, twice (yfrn, K2tog), K1,

Row 2: K2, yfwd, K2tog, K1, sl1, (K2, P1 into 2nd loop of yarn) twice.

Row 3: (yarn twice, K2tog) twice, sl1, K2, yfwd, K2tog, K2, and K1.

Row 4: (K2, P1) twice, K4, yfwd, K2tog, K1, sl1, (K2, P1) twice.

Row 5: (yarn twice, K2tog) twice, sl1, K2, yfwd, K2tog, K4, and K1.

Row 6: (K2, P1) twice, K6, yfwd, K2tog, K1, sl1, (K2, P1) twice.

Row 7: sl1, K2, yfwd, K2tog, K6, (yarn twice, K2tog) twice, K1, (yfwd, K2tog) twice.

Sl1, (K2, P1) twice, K8, yfwd, K2tog, K1, on row eight.

Row 9: sl1, K2, yfwd, K2tog, K8, (yarn twice, K2tog) twice, K1, (yfwd, K2tog) twice.

Sl1, (K2, P1) twice, K10, yfwd, K2tog, K1, in row 10.

Sl1, K2, yfwd, K2tog, K15 in row 11.

Bind off 10 stitches, K6, yfwd, K2tog, and K1 in row 12.

Do these 12 rows again.

- Edging openwork (top section of picture)
- Dioxide trimming (middle section of the image)
- Lacy cutting (bottom area of view)

Edging OPENWORK

Add 5 stitches.

Row 1: K2tog, sl1, yfwd, yfwd, K2, (RS)

Sl1, K to finish in row 2 and all WS rows.

Row three: sl1, thrice (yfwd, K2tog), yfwd, K1.

Sl1, twice (yfwd, K2tog), yfwd, K2 in row 5.

Row 7: sl1, three times (yfwd, K2tog), yfwd, K1.

Row 9: Sl1, 3 times (yfwd, K2tog), yfwd, K2.

Bind off six stitches in row 11, then knit two stitches together to form a square before incorporating one.

Row 12: K.

Do these 12 rows again.

DIOXIDE trimming

Add 10 stitches.

K5, K2tog, yfwd, K3tog in Row 1 (RS).

yrn to M1, K to finish in row 2 and all WS rows.

K4, K2tog, yfwd, K1, yfwd, K2tog in row three.

K3, K2tog, yfwd, K3, yfwd, K2tog in row 5.

K2, K2tog, yfwd, K5, yfwd, K2tog in row 7.

K4, yfwd, K2tog, K1, K2tog, yfwd, K3tog in row nine.

K5, yfwd, K3tog, K3tog, yfwd; row 11; row 12; as row 2.

Do these 12 rows again.

Cast on 18 stitches for LACY edging

Row 1: K6, P7, and K5 (WS).

Row 2: (yfwd, K1) twice, sl1, K2, yfwd, K2tog, K2, K2tog, yfwd, K5, yfwd, K2tog.

K6, yfwd, K2tog, P7, K2, yfwd, K2tog, and K1 make up row three.

Row 4: sl1, K2, yfwd, K2tog, K1, (K2tog, yfwd) twice, K4, yfwd, K2tog, (yfwd, K1) twice, K2, (K2tog, yfwd) twice.

K8, yfwd, K2tog, P7, K2, yfwd, K2tog, K1 make up row 5.

Row 6: Sl1, K2, yfwd, K2tog, 3 times (K2tog, yfwd), K3, yfwd, K2tog, twice (yfwd, K1), K4.

Row 7: P7, K2, yfwd, K2tog, K1, K10, and K2tog.

Row 8: sl1, K2, yfwd, K2tog, K1, (yfwd, K1) twice, K4, yfwd, K2tog, and K6.

Bind off 8 stitches, then in Row 9: K3, yfwd, K2 tog, P7, K2, yfwd, K2 tog, K1.

Rows 2 through 9 should be repeated.

- Berry trimming (top section of picture)
- Edge of fan (middle section of the image)
- A spray edge (bottom area of view)

BERRY trimming

Add 4 stitches.

Row 1: K2, yfwd, K2 (RS).

K in rows 2, 4, and 6.

K3, yfwd, K2 in row 3.

K2, yfwd, K2tog, yfwd, K2 in row 5.

K3, yfwd, K2tog, yfwd, K2 in row seven.

Bind off 4 stitches in row 8 and knit to the end.

Repeat these 8 rows.

Edge of FAN

Add 13 stitches.

Row 1: K1, yfwd, K2tog, K5, sl1, K1, yfwd, K2tog, K2, (RS)

yrn to M1, K2tog, K to end in row 2 and all WS rows.

Row 3: sl1, K1, yfwd, K2tog, K4, twice (yfwd, K2tog), yfwd, K2, K4.

sl1, K1, yfwd, K2tog, K3, (yfwd, K2tog) three times, yfwd, K2, row five.

Row 7: sl1, K1, (yfwd, K2tog) four times, K2, yfwd, K2, (yfwd, K2tog), K2.

Row 9: sl1, K1, (yfwd, K2tog) five times, yfwd, K2, (yfwd, K2tog), K1.

Row eleven: sl1, K1, yfwd, K2tog, K1, K2tog, (yfwd, K2tog) five times, K1.

Row 13: sl1, K1, (yfwd, K2tog) four times, K2, K2tog, and K1.

Row 15: sl1, K1, (yfwd, K2tog) three times, K3, K2tog, and K1.

sl1, K1, yfwd, K2tog, K4, K2tog, (yfwd, K2tog) twice, K1, row 17.

Row 19: K1, K5, K2tog, yfwd, K2tog, K1, sl1, K1, K2tog.

As in row 2, row 20.

20 rows of repetitions.

A SPRAY edges

Add 11 stitches.

Row 1: (RS) sl1, K2, yfwd, P2tog, YRN, SKP, twice (yfwd, SKP).

Row 2: [P1, (K1, P1) into next st] three times, P2, yarn, P2tog, K1 tbl.

Sl1, K2, yarn, P2tog, K10 in row three.

Sl1, P11, yarn, P2tog, K1 tbl in row 4.

Sl1, K2, Yfrn, P2tog, K10 in row 5.

Bind off 4 stitches in each row, P7, yarn, P2tog, and K1 tbl in row 6.

Repetition: 6 rows.

- A diamond lace border (top section of picture)
- Edging using loop and braid (middle section of picture)
- Godma's cutting (bottom area of image)

A DIAMOND LACE border

Add 9 stitches.

K for row one and all RS rows.

K3, K2tog, yfwd, K2tog, yfwd, K1, yfwd, K1; Row 2.

K2, K2tog, yfwd, K2tog, yfwd, K3, yfwd, and K1 in row 4.

Row 6: K5, yfwd, K1, K2tog, yfwd, K2tog, yfwd.

Row 8: K1, K2tog, yfwd, K2tog, K3, yfwd, K2tog, K2tog.

K4, yfwd, K2tog, yfwd, K3tog, yfwd, K2tog for row 10.

K5, yfwd, K3tog, yfwd, K2tog in row 12.

Do these 12 rows again.

Edging using LOOP AND BRAID

Add 6 stitches.

Row 1 (RS): K2, yfrn, K2, yfwd, K1, K2tog.

Row 2: K1, (K1, P1) into yfrn, P2tog, yfwd, K3; K1.

K1, K2tog, yfwd, K5 in row three.

Row 4: P2tog, yfwd, K3, bind off 2 stitches.

Repeat these 4 rows.

GODMA'S cutting

Add 20 stitches.

(RS) K in Rows 1, 3, 5, 7, and 9.

Row 2: Sl1, K3, 7 repeats of (yfwd, K2tog), yfwd, K2, Sl1.

Row 4: Sl1, K6, 6 times (yfwd, K2tog), yfwd, K2.

Row 6: sl1, K9, 5 repetitions of (yfwd, K2tog), yfwd, K2.

Row 8: sl1, K12, 4 repeats (yfwd, K2tog), yfwd, K2.

10th row: sl1, K23.

Row 11: K20, bind off 4 stitches.

Rows 2 through 11 should be repeated.

- A LEAF's edge (left section of picture)
- A CABLE's edge (middle section of the image)
- SERRATED border (right area of view)

A LEAF's edge

Add 6 stitches.

Row 1: K3, yfwd, K1, K2, and K2 (RS).

Row 2: P6, K1, inc1

K2, P1, K2, yfwd, K1, yfwd, K3, K2 in row 3.

P8, Inc. 1 K, K2, Row 4.

K2, P2, K3, yfwd, K1, yfwd, K4, K2 on row 5.

Row 6: P10, K1, P3, and K3.

K2, P3, SKP, K5, K2tog, K1 in row seven.

Row 8: P8, K1, P1, K3, inc1.

K2, P1, K1, P2, SKP, K3, K2tog, K1 in row nine.

Row 10: P6, K1, P1, K3, inc1 P.

K2, P1, K1, P3, SKP, K1, K2tog, K1 in row 11.

Row 12: P4, K1, K2, P1, K3, inc1 P4.

K2, P1, K1, P4, SK2P, K1 on row 13.

P2tog, bind off 3 stitches, K1, P1, K3, row 14.

Repetition: 14 rows.

A CABLE's edge

Add 8 stitches.

Row 1: P3, K4, P1, (RS).

Row 2: P4, K3, K1, P4.

P1, P3, C4F, Row 3.

Row 4: P4, K3, K1, P4.

Repeat these 4 rows.

SERRATED border

Add 8 stitches.

Row 1: K to last two stitches, inc. 1, yfwd, sl1.

Row 2: K1, SKP, K1, twice, yfwd, sl1, K1, tbl, K1.

K1 tbl, K to end, turn, and cast on 3 stitches in row 3.

Row 4: K1, K1, K2, (yfwd, SKP, K1) twice, K1, yfwd, and sl1.

K1 tbl, K to last 2 stitches, inc 1 K, yfwd, sl1 in row 5.

Row 6: K1, yfwd, SKP, K1, sl1, K1 tbl, inc1 K, K2, (yfwd, SKP, K1) 3 times.

K1 tbl, K to final 2 stitches, K2tog in row 7.

Row 8: (Yfwd, SKP, K1) twice, SKP twice, K4 twice, yfwd, sl1.

As in row 7, row 9.

Row 10: K1, yfwd, SKP, yfwd, sl1, K2, yfwd, SKP, bind off 3 stitches.

Rows 3 through 10 should be repeated.

4.5 Decorative stitches

This assortment delivers the more theatrical type of texture of stitch designs. There are numerous larger bobbles in various arrangements and embossed bells and leaves, some of which are well known for adorning Aran designs. More ornate textures come in the form of wildly voluminous loops, enormous faux wires, and substantial smocked patterns.

Although the growth of your knitting will probably be relatively slow, it is not difficult to create these decorative stitches. However, some of them have a serious yarn addiction. The results, though, are undeniably striking and well worth the effort.

- Scrap stitch (left section of picture)
- Stitch popcorn (middle section of the image)
- Brown nut stitch (right section of the image)

SCRAP stitch

Multiples of 6 stitches plus 5 stitches produce a bobble: knit into the front and back of the same stitch twice;

(turn and P5; turn and K5; lift 2nd, 3rd, 4th, and 5th stitches over the first stitch and off RHN).

1st row: (RS) K.

All WS rows except row 2: P.

Row 3: K.

Row 5: K5, bob, K5, repeat from beginning to end.

Row 7: K.

Row 9: K.

Row 11: K2, form a bobble, K5, repeat from the last stitch to the third stitch, K3.

Row 12: P.

Do these 12 rows again.

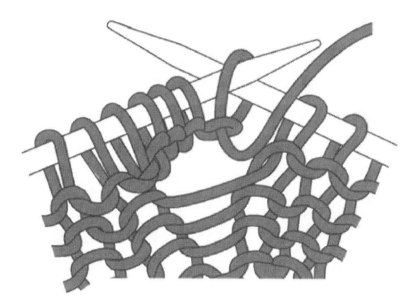

Bobble stitch 1. Knit twice into the front and rear of the following stitch before incorporating it into the front one more.

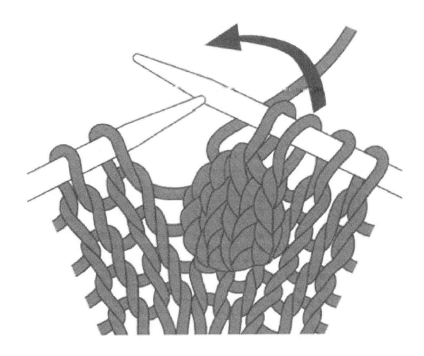

Two-bounce stitch to finish the bobble, lift the second, third, fourth, and fifth stitches over the first and of the RHN.

STITCH POPCORN

6 stitches plus 3 multiples

1st row: (RS) K.

P on row 2 and every WS row.

Row 3: K1, (K1, P1, K1) into the next st, pull the second and third stitches over the first stitch, and K5.

K2 in the last two stitches.

Row 5: K.

Row 7: K4, (P1, K1) into the next stitch, hoist the second and third stitches over the first stitch, K5, rep.

K5 from the last 5 stitches.

Row 8: P.

Repeat these 8 rows.

BROWN NUT stitch

Numerous 4 stitches plus three

Row 1: P3, (K1, yfwd, K1) into the next stitch, rep from there until the last 3 stitches, P3.

Row 2: K3, P3, K3, continue to the end.

Row 3: P3, K3, repeat from last three stitches, P3.

K3, P3tog, K3, rep from beginning to end in row 4.

Row 5: P.

Row 6: K.

Row 7: P3, repeat from * to the final 2 stitches (K1, yfwd, K1) in the next stitch, P1.

Next stitch (K1), P1.

Row 8: P3, K3, repeat from last four stitches, K1, P3, K1.

P1, *K3, P3, repeat from * until the last 4 stitches, K3, P1. Row 9:

Row 10: K1, P3tog, K3, rep from the first stitch to the final four stitches, K1.

Row 11: P.

Row 12: K.

Do these 12 rows again.

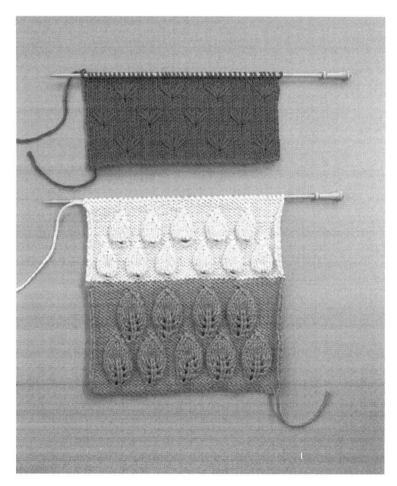

- Dotted stitch (top section of picture)
- Motif bell (middle section of the image)
- Emblazoned leaf pattern (bottom section of picture)

Dotted stitch

10 st. multiples plus 8

make daisy: K into the loop on left-hand needle three rows below the second stitch, draw up a loop, (K2, pull

Rows 1, 3, and 5: (RS) K. following loop through the same stitch twice.

P for rows 2, 4, and 6.

Row 7: K2, create a daisy; *K6, create a daisy; repeat from * to the last 2 stitches; K2.

P2, P2tog, P1, twice, P2tog, P5, repeat from * to final 9 stitches in row eight (P2tog, P1)

3 times.

K for rows 9, 11, and 13.

10, 12, and 14th rows: P.

K7, *make daisy, K6, rep from * to last stitch, K1, row 15.

P2, *P5, (P2tog, P1) twice, P2tog, rep from * to the final 6 stitches, P6, complete row 16.

Do these 16 rows again.

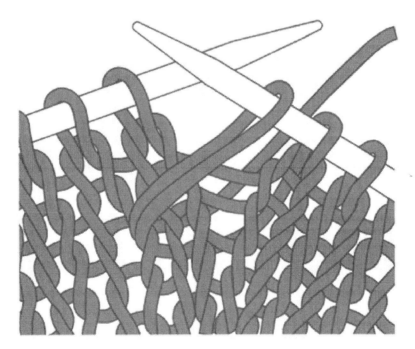

Knit into the loop three rows below the second stitch.

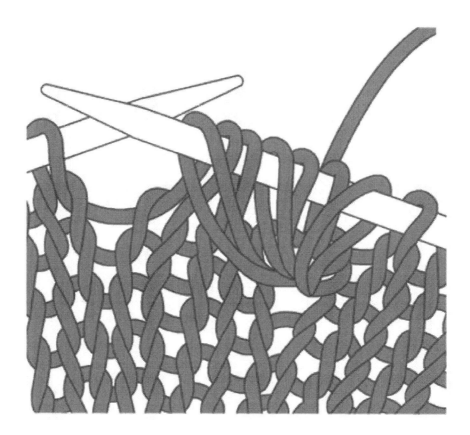

Work three long loops for the daisy, knitting two stitches between the loops.

MOTIF BELL

a 6-stitch motif on a reverse stitch backdrop

P to cluster position, cast on 6 stitches, and P to end in row 1 (RS).

K backdrop, P cast-on cluster, K to end for row 2 and all WS rows.

Row 3: K cluster, P to end, P backdrop.

P background, SKP, K2, K2tog, and P to end in row 5.

Row 7: P to start, SKP to the middle, K2tog to end.

Row 9: K2tog in the middle, P at the end.

P background, P2tog, P to end in row 11.

Row 12: K.

Do these 12 rows again.

Emblazoned leaf pattern

9 stitches in a row on a reverse stitch backdrop

Row 1: (RS) P to end, yon, K1, yarn, P to leaf position

K backdrop, P cast-on cluster, K to end for row 2 and all WS rows.

Row 3: P for the backdrop, K1, twice (yfwd, K1), P until the end.

Row 5: K2, yfwd, K1, yfwd, P backdrop, K2, P to end.

Row 7: P in the foreground, K3, yfwd, K1, yfwd, and K3, P to the end.

Row 9: P in the foreground, SKP, K5, K2tog, and P to the end.

Row 11: P in the foreground, SKP, K3, K2tog, and P to the end.

P backdrop, SKP, K1, K2tog, P to finish in row 13.

P backdrop, SK2P, P to end in row 15.

Row 16: K.

Do these 16 rows again.

KNOTTED MOCK cable

Cable with knots

30 stitches in a row on a reverse stitch backdrop.

Two safety pins and an extra needle are needed.

Row 1: P6, (P2, K1 tbl twice), (RS) (K1 tbl twice, P2) 3 times, P6.

Row 2: K2, P1 tbl twice, K2, K6, (P1 tbl twice, K2, K2) three times.

Replicate rows 1 and 2 seven more times in rows 3–16. Work the tangled cable next.

(K1 tbl twice, P2 twice, K1 tbl twice) is the first step. Keep the remaining stitches on the extra needle.

11 further rows are completed after turning the work. Keep stitching on safety pin A.

Step 2: Leave the subsequent 10 reverse stitch sts on a spare needle in the rear of the piece.

3. Join the yarn to the last group of stitches. Work 20 rows in a row pattern. Keep stitching on safety pin B.

Step 4: To tie a knot, cross the left rib (B) over and under the right rib (A).

Step 5: Attach the rib A, rib B, and reverse st stitches to the LHN.

Rows 17–24: Repetition of Rows 1 and 2.

Repeat this 24 times.

BOBBLE brocade

6 stitches plus 2 multiples

(RS) P2, *K1, P2, rep from * until the end of the row.

K2, *P1, K2, repeat from * to the end in row 2.

P2, *K1, P2, (P1, K1, P1, K1) into the next stitch, P2, repeat from * to the end of the row.

K2, *P4, K2, P1, K2, repeat from * until the end of the row.

P2, *K1, P2, K4, turn and K4, turn and P4, P2, repeat from * until the end of the row.

K2, *P4tog, K2, P1, K2, rep from * to the end for row 6.

As in row 1, row 7.

As in row 2, row 8.

P2, *(P1, K1, P1, K1) into the next stitch, P2, K1, P2, repeat from * to the end of row 9.

K2, *P1, K2, P4, K2, repeat from * until the end of the row.

P2, *P4, turn and K4, turn and P4, P2, K1, P2, repeat from * to the end of row 11.

Row 12: P1, K2, P4tog, K2, *P1, K2, rep from * to end.

Do these 12 rows again.

HOLLOW OAK with bobbles

15 stitches in a row on a reverse stitch backdrop.

Make a bobble by knitting twice into the same stitch's front and back.

Lift the second, third, fourth, and fifth stitches over the first stitch (turn and P5, then turn and K5).

First Street and RHN

T3B = K2, P1 from CN, slip first onto CN and hold at back of work.

T3F = P1, K2 from CN, 2 sts onto CN and hold at the front of work.

(WS) K5, P5, K5 in Rows 1, 3, 5, and 7.

Row 2: Make a bobble, P5, K2, K2, and P5.

Row 4: Make a bobble with P5, K3, and P5.

As in row 2, row 6.

Row 8: P1, T3F, T3B, P4, and P4.

K4, P2, K1, P1, K1, P2, K4 in row nine.

Row 10: P3, K1, P1, K1, T3F, P3, T3B.

K3, P3, K1, P1, K1, P3, K3 in row 11.

Row 12: P1, K1, P1, T3F, P2, T3B, (P1, K1) twice.

Row 13: K2, P2, 3 times (K1, P1), K1, P2, K2.

P2, K3, (P1, K1) twice, P1, K3, P2. Row 14

As row 13, row 15.

Row 16: P1, K1 twice, P1, T3B, P2, T3F.

As row 11, row 17.

P3, T3F, K1, P1, K1, T3B, P3, row 18

Like row 9, row 19.

P1, T3B, T3F, P4, and row 20: P4.

20 rows of repetitions.

DARK honeycomb

12 stitch multiples plus 1

Wrap yarn twice counterclockwise around the next five stitches before tying off.

from CN, (K1, P3, K1)

Row 1: (RS) 3 times (K1, P3), K1.

WS rows 2 through all: (P1, K3) three times, P1.

Tie 5, P3, tie 5, row 3.

as in row 1, row 5.

K1, P3, tie 5, P3, in row 7

As in row 2, row 8.

Repeat these 8 rows.

WHEATEAR pattern

15 stitches in a row on a reverse stitch backdrop.

Make a bobble by knitting twice into the same stitch's front and back.

Lift the second, third, fourth, and fifth stitches over the first stitch (turn and P5, then turn and K5).

First Street and RHN

T3B = K2, P1 from CN, slip first onto CN and hold at back of work.

T3F = P1, K2 from CN, 2 sts onto CN and hold at the front of work.

(WS) K5, P5, K5 in Rows 1, 3, 5, and 7.

Row 2: Make a bobble, P5, K2, K2, and P5.

Row 4: Make a bobble with P5, K3, and P5.

As in row 2, row 6.

Row 8: P1, T3F, T3B, P4, and P4.

K4, P2, K1, P1, K1, P2, K4 in row nine.

Row 10: P3, K1, P1, K1, T3F, P3, T3B.

K3, P3, K1, P1, K1, P3, K3 in row 11.

Row 12: P1, K1, P1, T3F, P2, T3B, (P1, K1) twice.

Row 13: K2, P2, 3 times (K1, P1), K1, P2, K2.

P2, K3, (P1, K1) twice, P1, K3, P2. Row 14

As row 13, row 15.

Row 16: P1, K1 twice, P1, T3B, P2, T3F.

As row 11, row 17.

P3, T3F, K1, P1, K1, T3B, P3, row 18

Like row 9, row 19.

P1, T3B, T3F, P4, and row 20: P4.

20 rows of repetitions.

DARK honeycomb

12 stitch multiples plus 1

Wrap yarn twice counterclockwise around the next five stitches before tying off.

from CN, (K1, P3, K1)

Row 1: (RS) 3 times (K1, P3), K1.

WS rows 2 through all: (P1, K3) three times, P1.

Tie 5, P3, tie 5, row 3.

as in row 1, row 5.

K1, P3, tie 5, P3, in row 7

As in row 2, row 8.

Repeat these 8 rows.

Chapter 5
BEGINNER PATTERNS

5.1 Classic Chunky Cowl

Nowadays, cowls are popular, and Laura Bain created this simple Pattern from Red Heart. Use a variegated yarn and numerous different colors of crochet hooks to make this Pattern for a Different style. Check out the video link in the Pattern if you haven't already.

- Two size Q balls of Red Heart Grande in Foggy are required (16mm)
- A tapestry needle for weaving in the ends and a crochet hook. This hat
- When finished, it will be approximately 8 inches by 34 inches.
- The gauge is 6 stitches and 3 rows to 4 inches for this item.
- Chain 12

Row 1 (right side): Double crochet starting with the third chain from the hook. Initial Double Crochet does not count), then in each chain across, 10 double crochets in a row.

Chain 2 for Row 2. (Does not count as Double Crochet here and throughout), Double crochet across, turning after each double crochet.

Until the piece is 33 inches long or the desired length, repeat Row 2.

Bringing Rows Together: Holding the first and end rows' incorrect sides together Chain 1 and single crochet in each Double after working through both thicknesses

10 sc in crochet.

Trim off.

FINISHING

Integrate ends

5.2 Single Square Coasters

How adorable are these? It's possible to construct these Granny Square coasters in various colors, and they'd make wonderful stocking stuffers or gifts for newlyweds. This is a fantastic idea to finish your stockpile and make some entertaining house decor.

You will need three balls of Red Heart Gumdrop in Cherry (Color A), Turquoise (Color B), and Lilac to complete the coasters shown (Color C).

Additional materials are needed for a tapestry needle and a crochet hook in size G/6 (4.25 mm). When finished, each square will be four inches square.

Color progression:

color progression

Coaster 1: Color B is used for all four rounds.

Rounds one and two of Coaster Two are worked in Color A, while Rounds three and four are worked in Color B.

Rounds 1 and 2 are worked in Color A on Coaster Three, while Rounds 3 and 4 are performed in Color C.

When making the granny squares, you will be working in rounds.

Two sets of three double crochet clusters will be done in each corner, and each group will be performed in the chain three space from the previous game. Make a slip knot and attach it to your hook whenever the design instructs you to join a new color. Pull the yarn through the stitch and the loops on your turn after inserting the hook into the proper stitch. The pattern does not count this as a stitch.

Chain 4 starts each square, then stitch the first chain to form a ring.

Round 1 (right side): Chain 3 (counts as dc here and throughout), 2 dc in ring, chain 3, 3 dc in ring; repeat from * twice, chain 3; join with a slip stitch on top of beginning chain-3 - 12 dc; 4 chain-3 spacing. Trim off.

Round 2: Chain 3, slip stitch in the up next 2 double crocheted and chain-3 gap, 2 double crochet, loop chain 3, 3 double crochets in the next chain-3 space; repeat from * twice; join with a slip stitch in the top of the starting chain-3. If your hair color changes, fasten off.

Round 3: Chain 3, (2 double crochet, loop chain 3, 3 double crochet) in the same chain-3 space, (3 double crochet, loop chain 3, 3 double crochet) in the next corner chain-3 space, slip stitch in the next 2 double crocheted and corner chain-3 space, or join next color with a slip stitch in any corner chain-3 space; repeat from * around, stopping the last repeat at *; join with a slip stitch on top of the first chain-3.

Round 4: Slip stitch in the space between the next two double crochets and the chain-3, chain 3, (2 double crochet, loop chain 3, 3 double crochet) in the same chain-3 space, [3 double crochet between up next two 3-double crochet groups] twice*, (3 double loop crochet, chain 3, 3 double crochet) in the next corner chain-3 space; repeat from * around, ending last repeat at *; join with a slip stitch on top of the chain-3 to begin. Integrate ends.

5.3 Fruit Platter Scarf

You can try your color-changing abilities with this lovely scarf pattern.

To tighten up your yarn, draw the new color through the two loops in the last stitch of the row until you have two loops on your hook. Turn your project over and carry with the pattern in the new hue.

Aqua (Color A), Kelly Green (Color B), Fern (Color C), Radiant Yellow (Color D), Raspberry (Color E), and Cheery Cherry are the colors of Vanna's Choice by Lion Brand (Color F). Vanna's Choice Baby Yarn is Cheery Cherry.

A tapestry needle and a crochet hook of size J/10 (6 mm) are also required for weaving in the ends.

22-link chain for Color A.

Row 1: Half double crochet starting with the second chain from the hook

Half double crochet each chain across, beginning with the third chain from the hook (the first two chains do not count as stitches), and you will have 20 stitches after Row 1.

Row 2: Half double crochet in each stitch across after a 2 chain (does not count as a stitch).

When the piece reaches 10 inches (25.5 cm), switch to B in the final stitch.

Repeat Row 2 by working 10 inches (25.5 cm) of each color block using B, C, D, E, and F, switching colors in the final stitch of each color block.

Trim off.

FINISHING

Integrate ends

5.4 Barefoot Sandals

They're so adorable! Imagine wearing your very own handcrafted barefoot sandal to the beach or the pool. These can be made with various yarn colors to fit your mood and attire. By slip sewing into the middle of the first chain three space, you first complete the ankle strap before forming the triangle shape of the sandal. The rows naturally get shorter, as a result, eventually coming to a point at the toes. Slide the button onto the yarn before beginning to crochet, and then slide it along as you go. When you crochet the buttonhole, it will be at the proper location. Measurement is not crucial for this project.

To weave in the ends, you'll need a tapestry needle, a size G/6 (4 mm) crochet hook, and one ball of lavender Lion Brand Micro spun Yarn.

Observation: If the garment is too lengthy for the foot, skip Row 8 by working a slip stitch to the middle of the second chain gap on Row 7. Row 9.

Chain 6, then join with a slip stitch to create a loop for a button.

Row 1: Chain 36, slide button to end of the row, single crochet across to ankle strap loop in the second chain from hook, finish crochet in a double chain from the angle, end of - 35 stitches.

Row 2: Single crochet on the 11th stitch from the final stitch of the previous row and in the next 14 or 15 stitches to attach the yarn.

Row 3: Chain 6 (counts as double crochet and a chain 3 space), [skip 1 stitch, double crochet in next stitch, chain 3] through — 8 double crochets and 7 chain spaces.

Row 4: Slip stitch to the first chain 3 space's center, chain 6 (counts as double crochet and a chain 3 space), dc in the center of the next chain 3 space, (chain 3, dc in the next chain 3 lengths) across, leaving the remaining stitches unworked — a total of 7 double crochets and 6 chain-space.

Repeat row 4 with 6 dc and 5 chain spaces in row 5.

Repeat row 4 with 5 dc and 4 chain spaces in row 6.

Repeat Row 4 with 4 DC and 3 chain spaces in Row 7.

Row 8: Slip stitch to the center of the first chain 3 space, chain 3 (counts as dc), and twice dc in the center of the following chain 3 spaces for a total of 3 dc.

Row 9: Single crochet in the middle dc and slip stitch in the first stitch.

Row 10: Turn and single crochet into itself.

Row 11:

* Turn.
* Single crochet in same stitch; chain 8.
* Slip stitch into the same stitch to form a toe loop.
* End row.

Ends are woven in

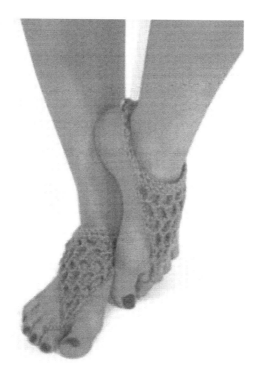

5.5 Afternoon Wrap

Kim Rutledge created this extremely lovely wrap for Caron Yarn spirations. The wrap is made using a four-row repeating pattern. The attractive wrap pattern is created by repeating this row pattern eight times.

The wrap will be 75 inches long and 20 inches broad when finished.

The following amounts of yarn are required:

Caron Simply Soft: 1 ball of Off White and 2 balls of Plum Perfect for Color B.

Caron All-Natural Heather for Color A, use 3 balls of Grey Heather and 1 ball of Charcoal Heather.

A tapestry needle and a crochet hook in size I/8 (5 mm) are also required for weaving in the ends.

Four pattern repeats are eight rows equal four inches in the wrap's gauge.

PATTERN FOR STITCHES (multiple of 3 stitches plus 1; plus 1 for foundation chain)

Row 1 (RS): Single crochet in the second chain from hook, double crochet in the third chain, skip the next couple chains, single crochet in the fourth chain, repeat across, turn.

Row 2: Chain 3 (counts as initial double crochet), double crochet in the first stitch, single crochet in next to last chain-3 space, chain couple, double crochet in second last single crochet, turn. Row 1: Chain 3, double crochet in the first stitch. Row 2: Chain 3, double crochet in second last chain-3 spaces.

Row 3: Chain 1, join with single crochet in the first stitch, chain 3, join with a double crochet in the next chain-2 space, and (single crochet, chain 3, double crochet) in the following chain-3 space; continue across, join with single crochet in the last double crochet (the turning chain), and turn.

The pattern is Rows 2 and 3, repeated.

A chain 224, WRAP.

Rows 1-3: Work 75 single crochets and 74 chain-2 spaces in Rows 1-3 of the Pattern Stitch.

Maintain pattern stitching while alternating colors as follows:

Repeat from the beginning for 4 more rows with A, 1 row with D, 2 rows with A, 2 rows with C, 4 more rows with B, 1 row with D, 4 more rows with B, 2 rows with C, 2 rows with A, 1 row with D, and 7 more rows with A.

Trim off. Weave all ends together using a yarn needle.

5.6 Easy Peasy Pompom Hat

Boy or female. The pattern depicts a young boy sporting a blue-themed hat, but you could just as easily use a young girl's preferred colors. The smallest size of the way is intended to fit a baby's head (3/6 (6/12-18/24) months). It is in parentheses greater lengths. The hat is created in one piece, then folded over and sewn at the top and side seams to form the cap. You can give any child in your life a cute look by adding a pompom to each corner.

12 single crochets and 13 rows equal four inches in the hat's gauge.

You will need one skein of Caron Charming Baby Ombre fabric in Sailor Boy Variegated and a crochet hook of size J/10 (6 mm). In order to secure the openings and stitch in the thread ends, a tapestries needle is also necessary.

Chain 47 (56-61).

Starting with a single crochet, work into the next strand from the hook on the first row. Single crocheting in each loop till the end of the chain. You should have 46 (55-60) single crochet rows.

Row 2: Chain 1. Until the row's conclusion, make 1 single crochet in every single crochet.

Third row: Chain 1, then make 1 single crochet and 2 double crochets in the first single crochet. Skip the next two single crochets. Make 1 single crochet and 2 double crochets in the single crochet. Repeat the previous three single crochets. Skip the next two single crochets. Adding one single crochet after the previous one. Fourth row: Chain 1; make 1 single crochet and 2 double crochets in the first single crochet. Skip the next two double crochets. In the double crochet after, make 1 single and 2 double crochets. Repeat the previous single crochet. Adding one single crochet after the previous one. Turn.

Repeat the last row until the work from the beginning measures 6 (or 7-8) inches. Fasten \off.

Piece folded in half. Sew the top and side seams.

Pompom (make 2).

50 or so times around three fingers with yarn. Remove from fingers, then bind firmly in the middle. Cut the loops on both sides. Trim to a round, smooth form. Sew a pompom to the hat's four top corners.

Recall to unwind and enjoy yourself. Don't feel you have to use the exact yarn brand or colors that the design specifies; instead, let your originality emerge. To assist you in learning the stitches and techniques I included in this book, I've provided several video links. You will also discover a helpful list of crochet resources to further your exploration of the fascinating crochet world. Once again, thanks, and keep fishing!

Specialty Crochet Methods

Several distinctive crochet techniques have developed and grown widely enough to carve out their markets. Some methods, such as Polish star, intermeshing, and Bruges lace, only use common crochet hooks. Others, like broomsticks and hairpin lace, started by using some ordinary household materials and a crochet hook. As soon as these techniques gained popularity, manufacturers created specialized instruments to take the place of the broomstick and hairpin.

5.7 Tapestry Tunisian

Tunisian crochet makes a wonderful visual canvas.

Images can be included in Tunisian crochet in two different ways: during crocheting or embroidery. Cross stitch is the ideal approach to add detail because basic Tunisian produces a largely square grid.

These amusing children's vests by Julia Bryant demonstrate two alternative techniques for depicting images in Tunisian crochet. Walter Whale was cross-stitched on a solid background stitched in Simple Tunisian Stitch. Delilah Duck was crocheted into the fabric in the manner of knitted intarsia, using various yarn colors as directed by the pattern grid (page 232). Either pattern can be incorporated into the cloth or done in cross stitch.

YOU WILL NEED Yarn Two 50 g balls of sport-weight yarn in Color A and MC, as well as small amounts of two contrast colors in Band C and black yarn for the eyes.

Hooks

• 4/E (3.5 mm) and 6/G (4 mm) crochet hooks for Afghans

Notions

• Gauge for tapestry needles

• 24 stitches and 20 rows equal 4 inches (10 em)

Size

• 2 years (4 years)

• Finished chest size: [66 (71) em] 26" (28").

• 12" from shoulder in length (13 34 ") [30.5 (35) em]

Notes: For either design, you can either work the cloth plain and cross-stitch the design on top of it, or you can intarsia the design into the fabric. One stitch or one row of Simple Tunisian Stitch corresponds to one square on the graph (page 232) (forward and return passes)

Back

Chain 73 (79) stitches with an Afghan hook and MC.

Work 30 (35) rows in TSS, using MC and color A, and place the stripes according to the chart for the back. Bind off the final 6 (7) stitches in TSS as you continue to shape the armhole and neck as shown on the chart. Fasten off the left front (cross-stitch version) in 37 (40) stitchcs using an afghan hook and MC chain.

Work 35 rows total in TSS. Do front for Walter Whale in me.

Delilah Duck should arrange her stripes according to the Left Front chart, using MC and color A. Bind off the final 6 (7) stitches while continuing in TSS and using the chart for shaping the neck and armholes. Trim off.

Front Right

37 (40) stitches with an afghan hook and MC chain.

Work 30 (35) rows in TSS, using MC and color A, and follow the chart for stripe placement. Bind off the final six (7) stitches while continuing in the fundamental Tunisian crochet pattern and using the chart to shape the armholes and neck. Trim off.

Finishing

Place the pieces wrong sides together and, using MC yarn and a 4/E crochet hook, single crochet through both thicknesses to attach the shoulder and side seams.

Edging

Row 1: Attach the MC to the lower edge at the right side seam with the 4/E hook and the right side facing. Single crochet all around with 3 single crochets in a corner, 59 (68) single crochets up right front to shoulder, 30 (30) single crochets along neck edge, 59 (68) single crochets down left front to bottom corner, 3 single crochets in the corner, 29 (31) single crochets across the bottom of left front, and 60 (65) single crochets across the bottom of the back.

To start the first sc, join with SI st. Trim off.

Row 2: With the right side facing, attach the MC to the previous round›s joining stitch with a 4/E hook. Work one single reverse crochet in each sc around, inserting two stitches in each corner stitch. Affix your SI st. Trim off.

Sleeve Edging

Row 1: With the right side facing, join the MC to the underarm seam with a 4/E hook, ch 1, and 1 sc in the same location. Then, work 68–74 sc evenly spaced around the armhole. SI st to first sc, join.

Trim off.

Row 2: Attach the MC to the joining chain with a 4/E hook while facing the right side. 1 reverse sc in each sc around, ch 1, 1 sc in the same spot. SI st to first sc, join. Trim off.

Embroidery

On the left front, stitch a cross-stitch pattern in the colors A, B, and C by utilizing one square of the afghan stitch for every cross-stitch.

Use black yarn to French knot an eye.

Color-Inlay Technique

Similar to a cross-stitched vest, make the back and right front.

Right Front

Chain 37 (40) chains with an afghan hook and MC. Using a bobbin for each color, stitch the stripes and design of your choice on the front.

(Cross the strands at the back to prevent a hole while changing colors.)

similar to the cross-stitched version's full vest.

5.8 One Piece, Top Down

The majority of dress patterns start at the bottom and move up. The fronts, back, and sleeves are made separately, then put together by sewing. Working from the top down and making the complete garment in one piece is another approach to crochet, which eliminates or drastically reduces the amount of finishing work required.

CHILD'S PULLOVER FROM THE TOP

You start at the neck and work down to the bottom to create this child's pullover. There are no seams to sew because it was crocheted in one continuous piece. The neck and shoulders are exercised continuously in the same direction in the circle. The rounds are done differently once you divide for the body and sleeves and start the shell pattern.

The end of each circle is joined to the beginning with a slip stitch, and the following round is started by turning and moving back oppositely. In the same way, each sleeve is worked in the competition.

(continued)

Child's Top-Down Pullover (continued)

YOU WILL REQUIRE

Medium-weight yarn

• Pictured is Lion Brand Cotton Ease, 3.5 oz (100 g)/207 yd (189 m), #134, which is made of 50% cotton and 50% acrylic. Terracotta: 3, 3, 4, and 4 skeins

Hook

• 8/H (5 mm)

Used stitches include chain, double crochet, and v-stitch.

• 4 clusters = 4”; • 12 dc = 4” (10 cm) (10 cm)

Sizes

• 2 (4, 6, 8)

• The final chest measurement 22” (25”, 28”, 30”) (56 [63.5, 71,76] cm)

Pullover

Notes:

1. To avoid a hole, work 1 linked dc (page 143) when you ch 3 to start the circle. At the end of the round, make 1 linked dc in the seam stitch.

Two stitches are added with each V-stitch increment.

Starting at the border of the neck, make a loose ch 43 (or use a larger hook if necessary to ensure that the opening fits over the child's head), be careful not to twist it, and then join it with a SI st to form a ring.

Ch 3 (counts as seam stitch at center back in the first round)

(Left Back Section), [1 dc, ch 1, 1 dc] in the following ch (V-st inc formed), and 1 dc in each of the next 7 ch.

[1 dc, ch 1, 1 dc] in the next 5 chains (Left Sleeve portion).

ch, 1 double crochet in each of the following 14 chains (front part), [1 dc, ch 1, 1 dc] in the next ch, and 1 dc in each of the next 5 ch (right Sleeve).

ch 1, 1 dc in the following section, 1 dc in each of the next 7

Link with a SI st to the top of the first ch-3 (Right Back portion) and ch.

There will be 5 dc in each Sleeve and 14 dc in the Front portion.

There will be 14 double crochets plus seam stitches in the back part.

Striated in a V-shape.

Rnd 2: Ch 3, [1 dc, ch 1, 1 dc] in each of the following 8 dc, 1 DC in each of the following 7 DCs, [1 DC, ch 1, next V-st space 1 dc] in the next V-ch-1 st's gap, 1 dc in each of the following 16 dc, [1 dc, ch 1, 1 dc] in the next V-ch-1 st's gap, 1 dc in each of next 7 dc, [1 dc, ch 1, 1 dc] in the following V-ch-1 st's space, and To join the next 8 dc, add a SI stitch to the top of the first ch-3.

Ch3, 1 dc in each of the following 9 dc, [1 dc, ch 1, 1 dc] in the third round.

1 DC in each of the next 9 DC, [1 DC, ch 1, next V-st space 1 dc] in the next V-ch-1 st's gap, 1 dc in each of the following 18 dc, [1 dc, ch 1, 1 dc] in the next V-ch-1 st's gap, 1 dc in each of next 9 dc, [1 dc, ch 1, 1 dc] in the

following V-ch-1 st's space, and Each of the following 9 dc, join with a Sl st to the top of the first ch-3.

Rnd 4: Ch 3, [1 dc, ch 1, 1 dc] in each of the next 10 dc.

One double crochet in each of the next 11 double crochets, [1 dc, ch 1, 1 dc] in the next V-ch-1 st's slot, 1 dc in each of the next 20 dc, [1 dc, ch 1, 1 dc] in the next V-ch-1 st's slot, with 1 dc in each [1 dc, ch 1, 1 dc] in the first ch-1 space of the following V-st, the following 11 dc

Dc in each of the following 10 dc, joining with a Sl st at the top of the first ch-3.

Continue in this way, adding 8 stitches every round, until you have

Left Back: 17 (19,21,23) stitches, Left Side: 25 (29, 33, 37) stitches

Front: 25 (29, 33, 37) stitches, Sleeve: 34 (38, 42, 46) stitches

Right Back, 118 (134, 17 (19, 21, 23, 23) Sts on Right Sleeve 150, 166) dc with seam stitches and corner gaps added.

Separate for the body and sleeves

Shell and will be connected because of how the shell pattern is designed.

Along the center back seam, after which the circular was flipped.

Rnd 1: Ch 3, skip the first dc, and make 1 dc in each of the next 17 (19,21, 23) Left Back Stitches, Ch 2, (2, 3, 3L Skip the Following 25, (29, 33, 37) DC left Sleeve, 1 DC each of the following 34 (38, 42, 46)

Front dc, ch 2, (2, 3, 3L), skip the next 25, (29, 33, 37) dc.

1 crochet in each of the following 17 (19, 21, and 23) dc on the Right Sleeve Join with a Sl stitch to the first ch-3 space and turn 68 (76, 84, 92) sts.

Ch 3, 2 dc in same dc, shell foundation row for a second round.

1 Sl st in the next dc, skip the following 2 dc, *ch 3, 2 dc in the same

Dc, skip 2 dc, 1 Sl st in the next dc*, repeat from * to * all the way around.

Work [1 Sl st, ch 3, 2 dc] in the ch-space at the armhole, 1

Rep from * to * to the next ch-space at the armhole, Sl stitch in the following dc, ch 3, 2 dc in the ch-space, 1 Sl st in the subsequent dc, rep

Turn 24 (28, from * to * to finish, join with 1 sc in the beginning ch-3).

30 and 32 shells.

Ch3, 2 dc in the same stitch, *[Sl st, ch3, 2 dc] in the next

Connect with 1 sc at the top of the turning after repeating from * in ch-3 space.

Chi is turning.

Repeat Rnd 3 for the pattern until the body is 7" (7WI, 8", 8Y2")

End off at 18 [19, 20.5, 21.5"] cm from the armpit.

Sleeves (make 2)

Sleeves will be worked in rounds with joining and turning.

Similar to Body, Join the yarn at the ch-space in the armhole opening.

*Chapter 3; 2 dc in the same spot; skip the next 2 dc; SI stitch in the following dc, *ch 3, 2 dc in the same dc, skip 2 dc, and 1 SI st after that Repeat around the Sleeve opening in dc*, finishing with the last SI st.

Join with a SI stitch to the top of the additional ch-space at the underarm.

Begin with lines 3 through 9 (11, 12, and 13).

Continue with the body's established shell pattern till the sleeves, measures 7WI (8", 8WI, 9") (19, 20, 21, and 23 centimetres) from

End off with underarm.

Neck Tuck

Work the shell pattern after joining yarn at the center back seam stitch.

All over the neck's edge, using beg ch sts; yarn together at Center back seam, *ch 3, 2 dc in the same stitch, skip 2 stitches, 1 single stitch Rep from * in the next stitch, joining with a SI stitch at the base of the beginning.

Ch. 3, stop.

Blocking

Place on a cushioned surface, if necessary, mist with water, and

Shape with a pat. Avoid ironing.

5.9 Bruges Lace

Bruges lace is created by crocheting a straight piece of fabric with a few double crochet stitches and arches (or chain gaps) at either end. The hooks are connected to give the material the desired shape when crocheting the tape.

There are benefits to making Bruges Lace as opposed to making other types of handcrafted lace with crochet. Small Bruges Lace pieces that can be created separately from one another can be combined to form a larger item. Projects that are in progress are portable and can be worked on incrementally.

You will require:

Patons and yarn Brilliant, 1.75 oz (50 g)/166 yd, 69 percent acrylic, 19 percent nylon, and 12 percent polyester (152 m), 03005

White Two skeins of Twinkle.

Hook • 5/F (3.75 mm)

Chain, double crochet, unfinished double crochet, and unfinished triple crochet were the stitches employed.

Gauge: 10 rows of Bruges tape equals 4" (10 cm); 4 double crochets equal 34" (2 cm); nevertheless, the meter is not crucial for this creation.

Unusual abbreviations: Finished size: 5Y2" (14 cm) wide and 66" (167.5 cm) long

Incomplete crochet terms include unfinished double crochet and unfinished triple crochet.

Ch6, 4 dc in the sixth ch from the hook in row 1, turn.

Ch5 (arch), dc in each of the following 4 dc, turn (8 hooks on either side of the tape), repeat for rows 2 through 16.

141

Ch2, place hook in the adjacent arch, yo, draw through, yo four times, (insert hook in next turn, yo, draw through), repeat from row 2 to row 17 (joining row). [Yo, draw yarn through 2 loops twice]

Yo twice, [insert hook in next arch, yo, draw yarn through], 3 times (unf tr created). [Yo, draw across 2 loops] twice 2nd. The unfinished turn made; repeat from * to* 3 times. Again, with 7 loops on the hook, draw through just 3 of them [yo, pull through 2 loops]. Yo twice, draw through the final three loops, ch 2, turn, dc in each of the following four dc, turn (4 joinings made).

Ch5, dc in each of the following 4 dc, turn. Rows 18, 20, (tape rows):

Row 19: Ch 6, sc in the middle of the previous joining (between the second and third tr), ch 4, sc in the next free arch, ch 1, turn, 51 st into the second ch of the beginning ch-6, ch 2, dc in each of the following four dc, turn.

Row 21: Ch2, work 51 stitches, placing the hook in the first ch of Row 1 (beginning ch), ch2, turn, and dc in each of the following 4 dc.

Tape rows 22–33: Ch 5, dc in each of the following 4 dc, turn (6 arches outside the tape from the last joining).

Rep Row 17 in Row 34.

Tape rows 35, 37, and 39: Ch 5, dc in each of the following 4 dc, turn.

Row 36: Ch 6, sc in the middle of the previous joining (between the second and third tr), ch 4, sc into the next free arch, ch 3, turn, 51 stitches in the second ch of the beginning ch-6, ch 2, dc in each of the following four dc.

Ch2, sc into the opposite free arch, ch2, turn, and dc in each of the following 4 dc are the steps in row 38.

Row 40: Ch 2, dc into the opposing free arch, ch 2, turn, and dc in each of the following four dc.

Repeat Rows 34–50 until the piece measures 66" (167.5 cm) or desired length. Rows 41–50 (tape rows): Ch 5, dc in each of the following 4 dc, turn (5 arches outside the tape from the last joining).

Completing rows 34 and 35 of the rep.

Second row: Ch 6, sc into the center of the previous joining (between the second and third tr), ch 4, sc in the following free arch, ch 1, turn, 51 stitches in the second ch of the beginning ch-6, ch 2, unf dc in each of the next 4 dc, yo, draw through all 5 loops on the hook, turn, 51 stitches into the opposite free arch. Trim off.

5.10 Intermeshing Crochet

Row 2: Begin with the MC, *work 1 dc from the rear in the next MC dc, ch 1, 1 dc front in the next MC dc, rep from * across the row, ending with the last dc. Make sure the final DC is behind the ch 4 of the CC in the third chain of the ch 4 and turn the ch 4 around (4).

Row 3: Pick up CC and work in the back of the work, 1 dc in the first dc, *ch 1, sk 1, 1 dc in the next dc, rep from *to the end, with the last dc in the third ch of the ch4, ch 4, do not turn (5).

Row 4: Take the MC. Having the penultimate dc in the third ch of the ch 4, behind the CC chain, do a ch-4 rotation after each repetition of *1 dc next dc from front, ch 1, 1 dc next dc from back, ch 1. (6).

Pick up CC in Row 5 just like Row 3.

Row 6: Begin by picking up the MC. Repeat from *, placing the last dc in the third ch of the ch4 behind the CC chain. Ch4 turn.

Rep For the Basic Intermeshing Pattern, rows 3, 4, 5, and 6.

Chapter 6
HOW TO READ DIAGRAMS AND CHARTS

Each design is presented in this book in both written and graphical format for your convenience. Others like having everything written down in text format, while the majority of knitters prefer to use the graphical representations of the charts. Pick the pattern that works best for you in terms of comfort and enjoyment while you knit.

Charted patterns may seem to some knitters to be a mystery code consisting of illegible symbols arranged in a grid in an attempt to conceal their meaning. Once one is acquainted with the "grammar" and "vocabulary" of the knitting chart, it is not difficult to translate the knitting chart and its symbols, similar to the case with other languages.

6.1 Brief Grammar Explanation

A visual depiction of the reverse side of a knitted cloth is referred to as a knitting chart. One stitch is represented by each individual square on the grid, and one row of squares represents one row of stitches.

The charts are read in the same direction as the cloth is knit, starting at the bottom and working your way up, with the first row of the chart being at the bottom and the final row being at the top. When reading right-side rows, you go from right to leave, following the sequence in which the stitches appear on the left-hand knitting needle. In a chart, the following example demonstrates the sequence in which stitches will be worked for Row 1, which is a right-side row and represents the side of the cloth that will be shown to the public:

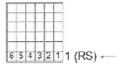

Naturally, if you're knitting back and forth in rows, when you reach the end of this first row and before beginning the next row, you flip your knitting so that the wrong side of the cloth is facing you. This is done before beginning the following row. The beginning stitch of this row will be the same stitch as the end stitch of the right-side row that you just finished knitting. This stitch will be considered the wrong-side stitch. As a result, wrong-side rows on charts are read in the other manner, from left to right, as is seen in the following example:

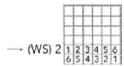

When crocheting in the round rather than going back and forth in rows, such as when knitting a cap or a pair of socks, the right side of the fabric will always be facing you. Because of this, you will read each row of the chart from right to left in these instances.

Certain patterns may be reversed and don't have definitive good or bad sides to them. In the majority of those designs, including Embossed Flow, I have chosen one of the sides at random to be the "right side." Other designs, such as Reversible Kerry Braids, on the other hand, have extensive cable work on both sides, which results in textiles that are as attractive on either side. There are two charts provided here for your knitting convenience. When working on Side A, you will refer to Chart A, and when working on Side B, you will refer to Chart B. Because there is no true "right" or "wrong" side to these patterns, the charts and all the symbols on them are read as if the rows were on the right side, moving from right to left. There is a very obvious indication of patterns that function in this manner.

The number of stitches required for a design may be quickly and easily determined with the use of knitting charts. This book makes use of a striking rectangular frame to denote the stitch repetition throughout the book. If additional stitches are needed on either side to center the pattern on the fabric, they will be indicated to the left or right of the repetition, depending on which side of the repeat they are on. For example, the Cross Hatch pattern has a multiple of ten stitches plus two stitches; it is a ten-stitch repetition with one "balancing" stitch on each side.

To read the chart below, for instance, you would begin in the bottom right-hand corner, read from right to left, work the four stitches inside the bold rectangle the number of times that are required to get across your fabric and finish the row with the stitch that is represented in this sample chart by the star. Because this stitch is not part of the stitch repeat, it only works once at the beginning of each row. It is the first stitch of every wrong-side row since wrong-side rows are read from left to right, and because right-side rows are read from right to left, it is always the final stitch of every right-side row.

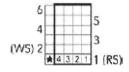

As you progress, you will notice that some of the charts, such as the leaf appliqué in Vineyard Lattice, for example, have irregular shapes rather than being rectangular, as is typically the case. This is because the book was designed to be used with the Vineyard Lattice crochet pattern. This is because the number of stitches in each row of the design does not remain the same; in order to generate variety and interest in the pattern, stitches are either added or removed.

Altering the number of stitches on a chart is handled in a different fashion by other charts. In certain patterns, such as the Caedmon Celtic Knot, the empty squares in the pattern "hold" the location of the stitches that were there before or that will ultimately be there.

When you come across these grey squares in the chart, you are not required to pay any attention to them;

consequently, the Comprehensive Stitch Key refers to them as "no stitch." It is important that you do not lose a stitch on your needles; instead, you should go on to the next symbol and the next stitch on your needles by skipping over the grey square.

In order to make some patterns "pop," they are created as panels or motifs on backgrounds that are kept relatively plain. Knit stitches on the right side and purl stitches on the wrong side to create a stockinette ground; to create a reverse stockinette ground, purl stitches on the right side and knit stitches on the wrong side.

6.2 The Words We Need to Know

The arrangement of symbols on a chart is what creates the stitch pattern, and each symbol on a chart will show how a stitch or collection of patterns will be worked after the chart is completed.

In most cases, the symbols have a visual appearance that is comparable to how the finished stitches would seem on the face of the knitted fabric that is visible to the public. For example, the sign for a knit stitch is a blank box, which shows the smooth look of a knit stitch; the indicator for a purl stitch is a dot, which depicts the ridged appearance of a purled stitch.

A symbol that takes up more than one square on the grid provides an indication of the number of stitches that are going to be engaged in a specific knitting technique. Because cables, for example, are stitched across more than one stitch, the symbols for cables fill numerous squares that are near to one another. You can instantly identify at a glance how many stitches are being crossed since the majority of the charts use a system in which each line or dot included inside a cable symbol symbolizes one of the stitches that are being crossed. As an illustration of a six-stitch wire, for instance, there would be three lines that crossed three other lines.

Even cable symbols have the appearance of the knitting techniques they stand for. The most prominent lines in the sign form a cross that extends to the left in a Left Cross, with the right-hand threads progressing in advance of the other stitches.

This should serve as a cue for you to position the cable needle that is holding those stitches in front of your work as you are knitting the symbol.

eft ross

Right Cross cable symbols, on the other hand, demonstrate the left-hand threads crossing over and traveling to the right of the other stitches. Because the stitches worked with the right hand seem to be following those worked with the left, you will need to slide them onto your cable needle and keep them behind the job you are doing.

ight ross

In a cable pattern, when one set of knit stitches passes over another set of knit stitches, the symbol for the cable will include diagonal lines to indicate the background stitches. If, on the other hand, the knit threads go over the purl stitches, the cable symbol will contain dots to depict the underlying stitches, as seen in the following image.

When following a pattern, if the directions tell you to hold the yarn or stitches in front or in back, this refers to the front or rear of the piece of work as it appears on your needles. The side that you are looking at is called the front, and the side that is away from you at that moment is called the back.

It goes without saying that multiple sets of symbols may be used to represent the same knitting operations by different designers and editors. However, these diverse sets of symbols are often variations on a theme; in general, all symbols look like the stitch that is produced. Just consider each one of them to be their own distinct "dialect" of this "strange language"! Since a key is located very close to each chart, deciphering them is often not too difficult.

The vast majority of the time, all rows in charts are shown exactly as they seem when seen from the front of the cloth. There are a few notable exceptions to this rule, such as reversible Dungourney Cables and Reversible Kerry Braids.

As a consequence of this, the identical sign may have a distinct meaning depending on whether it is found on the right side or the wrong side of a row. For example, a knit stitch on a right-side row is represented by a blank box. However, if you are working on a row with the wrong side facing you and you want the stitch to seem like a knit stitch on the other side of the cloth, you must purl it.

In the event that a symbol appears on both the right- and wrong-side rows of the chart, the Comprehensive Stitch Key will explain which knitting technique should be used where.

In most cases, working rows on the wrong side are not very difficult: you just knit the stitches that are currently shown on the knitting needle and purl the stitches that are now displayed on the knitting needle. Before you start knitting, read over the whole chart to make sure that this is the case, or you can simply look for the convenient symbol that is used throughout this book. If this is the case, you may speed through the rows on the wrong side by reading your knitting instead of the chart.

There are some publications that do not even show the rows on the charts that are on the incorrect side. Only odd numbers are used to label their rows on the right-hand side of their table. Because of this, while you are working on the wrong side of the row, you will simply knit the knits and purl the purls when you reach them.

I'm willing to wager that with some practice—and yes, a little bit of patience! —you'll find knitting from charts simple, quick, and even enjoyable.

6.4 Word-Form Knitting Instructions

Each stitched design in this book is presented in both chart and written form, with the understanding that some knitters are more comfortable following written instructions.

Instructions that are to be followed row by row are spelled out in numerical sequence. The rows that need to be repeated vertically will be marked at the conclusion of the design if the sequence has a repetition in this direction.

The "stitch multiple" is a term that refers to the number of stitches that are required to repeat the pattern throughout the whole width of the cloth, as was discussed before. The stitch repetition is indicated in the text guidelines by being written between an asterisk and a semicolon. To achieve symmetry, you must complete any stitches that fall outside of the asterisk and the semicolon.

For example, the Garter Rib row 1 instructions read like follows:

Row 1 (RS): *K5, p7, k4; repeat from the * across, ending with k1.

If you were to crochet this row, you would instead purl one crochet, then wrap one weave all the way throughout the row. When the row is finished, there will be one stitch remaining, and that stitch will be knitted.

In certain patterns, such as brocade, the amount of knit or reverse stitches is split up at both the beginning and end of the stitch repetition.

This pattern calls for beginning Row 1 with:

Row 1 (RS): *K1, p1; repeat from the * across, ending with k1.

This row can also be written as:

Row 1 (RS): K5, p7, *k9, p7; repeat from the * across, ending with k5.

Although their appearances may be different, the message they convey is the same: In order to knit this right-side row, you would first knit five stitches, then purl seven threads, and finally knit nine stitches (which would be the four stitches from the end of the repetition added to the five stitches that start the repeat). This book makes use of both ways of spelling out a row in an effort to strike a balance between clarity and convenience of use.

Certain patterns include portions of text that are enclosed in brackets similar to these []. Instructions pertaining to the stitches that are housed inside the brackets will come when they have been completed.

These brackets could suggest that a certain succession of stitches is expected to be done as a single stitch instead of being worked individually. For instance, in row 5 of "String of Pearls," the following is written:

Row 5: With B, k1, *[k1, yarn over, k1] all into the next st, slip the next st with the yarn in back; repeat from the * across, ending with k1.

Following the instructions between the parentheses means that after crocheting the first knot with Color B, you would perform all of the following into the next knot before taking the original stitch off the left-hand needle: Knit the stitch, then do a yarn over by wrapping the yarn more around a right-hand needle, and finally knit the stitch a second time by inserting the right-hand needle into the same stitch and knitting it once again. One single stitch may be used to create two additional stitches.

On other occasions, brackets are used to indicate a series of commands that will be repeated a particular number of times.

For instance, in Ribbed Squares, Row 9, you might write:

> **Row 9:** *P8, [k2, p2] twice; repeat from the * across.

> This row can also be written as:

> **Row 9:** *P8, k2, p2, k2, p2; repeat from the * across.

To complete this row, you will start by purling eight stitches, then knit two stitches, purl two stitches, knit two stitches, purl two stitches, and then continue this pattern all the way across the row, starting at the beginning. Abbreviations of conventional terms are used whenever possible within the directions of the design.

6.5 Diagrams v/s Charts

It's possible that you'll hear someone use the phrases "diagram" and "chart" interchangeably. However, even though this is true, schematics almost always relate to products that are crocheted in the round. Crochet designs that are worked in rows are often referred to as charts. Both kinds of patterns read in a way that is analogous to one another and make use of the same symbols.

How to Understand a Crochet Schematic

Diagrams are graphical representations of the crochet pattern that you are working on. Reading crochet diagrams should be done in a counterclockwise orientation, working from the center outward. Reading the symbols for each round should start in the middle and go clockwise around the board.

You can see how the pattern starts with eight chain stitches that are connected together with a slip stitch in the picture that follows. The following round starts with a double crochet into the same chain stitch as the beginning of the previous round, for a total of 4 chain stitches. After working a V-stitch into each chain stitch around, the V-stitch is linked into the third chain stitch of the initial chain of chain 4 to complete the pattern.

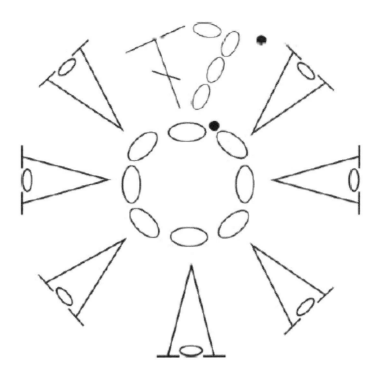

A slip stitch is worked into the gap created by the initial V-stitch, which was created by chaining 1. After that, chain 3 works a single crochet stitch into the gap created by the previous chain 1 of the following V-stitch.

Continue doing so until you approach the first chain 3 of the round, at which point you should insert your hook into the slip stitch that marked the beginning of the round. Remember to read it counterclockwise to crochet in the same direction as the diagram.

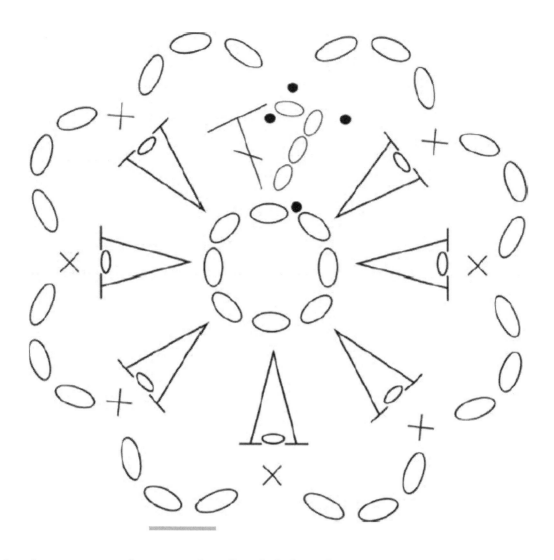

The solid dot that represents the connecting slip stitch from the previous round is the simplest method to locate the commencement of a round. If you look for this dot, you won't get lost. Some diagrams will include arrows pointing in the direction of the starting point, while others will not.

Proceed to work your way around the diagram in an anticlockwise fashion, ironing out the details as you go.

The schematic for this theme is finished looking like this. There are four rounds, and in order to link them, you will slip stitch at the end of each one. The beginning of the third round consists of chaining 3 and then working a cluster stitch into the first chain-3 gap. Make a single crochet into the next single crochet after chaining 3 first. Continue doing so all the way around the motif, and then connect with a slip stitch into the beginning chain stitch.

The fourth round starts with three single crochet stitches worked into the first chain-3 space, one single crochet stitch worked into the eye of the cluster stitch, and three single crochet stitches worked into the next chain-3 space, and one single crochet stitch worked into the following single crochet stitch. This step is repeated all the way around, and then you will link it to the initial single crochet using a slip stitch.

If you look at the diagram alongside these textual directions, you'll notice that if you follow the diagram, it will be much simpler for you to imagine how the finished product should appear.

6.6 Reading a Crochet Chart

In columns while starting at the bottom and working our way up. In most cases, the cornerstone chain is not counted as the initial row, and its presence on the chart is either uncertain or entirely absent.

Keep in mind that while reading charts, odd rows should be read from right to left, and even rows should be read from left to right. This will make reading the charts much simpler. As you crochet, start in the bottom right-hand corner of the pattern, then work your way up the chart following the rows. It is a good idea to use a highlighter, ruler, or some other method to mark the rows that you finish so that it is easier to keep track of where you are in the process. This will help you stay on track.

Here is an example of a straightforward chart. The rows are shown in a variety of colors to facilitate easier reading and comprehension. Reading will go from right to leave, starting with the first row.

Start with a chain of 3, then work a double crochet stitch into each chain stitch before turning your work.

The chain 4 marks the beginning of row 2, which is read clockwise from left to right. You will double crochet into the next stitch after skipping one stitch. Chain 1, then skip the next stitch and repeat a double crochet stitch into the following stitch throughout the row until you reach the final two stitches, and then add a double crochet stitch into each of those stitches.

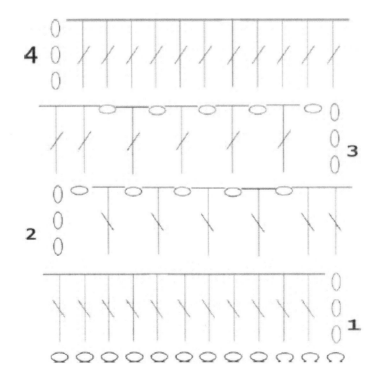

The chain 4 marks the beginning of row 3, which is read clockwise from right to left. You are going to skip the initial double crochet and then stitch double crochet into the space created by the previous chain 1 and then chain 1.

Continue working across the row until you reach the final two stitches, then double crochet into each of those stitches.

Make some adjustments to your work.

Chain 3 marks the beginning of row 4. Crochet a double stitch into each chain-1 gap and into each double crochet all the way across the row. Finish up by securing the tails and weaving them in.

There are a variety of patterns that employ charts. A chart may be used to work almost any pattern, provided that the pattern is worked in rows. Charts are helpful to me while I'm knitting or crocheting because they outline precisely where the stitches should go and give me an idea of what the finished product should look like as I work on it.

You will see a chart for a simple ripple design in the following illustration. Examine how well the chart corresponds to the real piece of crocheted cloth.

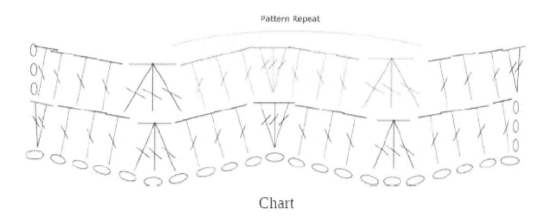

Chart

6.7 Pattern Repeats in Charts

If you look back at the earlier illustration of the ripple pattern, you'll see that there's a segment of the chart that's been labelled as a pattern repetition. Pattern repetitions are used by designers in charts in the same manner as they are in textual patterns. Charts are made simpler to read by using pattern repetitions, which display just a portion of each row rather than the complete row itself.

When you observe a pattern repeat on a chart, you should approach it the same way you would a pattern in textual form.

Start working from the spot where the repeating pattern begins and continue until you reach the point where it stops.

Now, navigate your way back to the start of the repetition on the chart, and make your way all the way through to the finish of the repeat an additional number of times.

If you had to write down the structure for the chart, it would look something like this: Ch sequences totalling 10 and 4

Row 1: dc into the fourth chain from the hook; dc into the next three stitches; dc3tog; dc into the next three stitches; 3dc into the next stitch; rep to the last stitch; 2dc into the last stitch; turn Row 2: chain 3, dc into the first stitch; dc into the next three stitches; dc3tog; dc into the next three stitches; 3dc into the next stitch; rep to the last stitch Keep repeating Row 2 until you reach the desired length.

Keep in mind that you should read the rows that include odd numbers from right to left and rows that contain even numbers from left to right. When reading a chart, you should always begin in the bottom right corner and work your way up.

6.8 How to Understand a Graphic and Knit

Coloring work and Fillet crochet both use graphs. They also serve as visual representations of crochet designs. When reading a chart, you should start in the bottom right corner and work your way up by reading the odd rows from right to left as well as even rows from left to right.

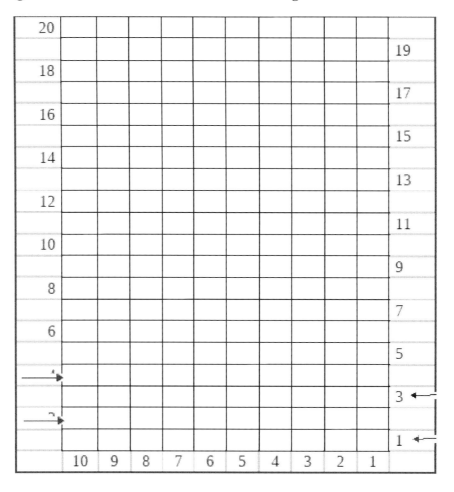

Depending on the sort of project you are working on, each square in a graph may represent either one stitch or a collection of stitches. If you are following an intarsia pattern, each square in the graph will represent either a single crochet stitch or a double crochet stitch in the color that is stated on the graph. In the technique known as "fillet crochet," each square may either be an open square consisting of one double crochet stitch and two chain threads or a filled square consisting of three double crochet stitches. The Corner-to-Corner method is yet another example of a technique that makes use of a chart. Each square on the chart denotes a particular color and a particular group of stitches that are utilized in the Corner 2 Corner pattern.

In most cases, a single chart may serve as a reference for many distinct kinds of methods. Here is an illustration of a straightforward heart graph.

		11	10	9	8	7	6	5	4	3	2	1		
←		■	■	■	■	■	■	■	■	■	■	■	9	←
→	8	■										■		
		■				■		■				■	7	←
→	6	■			■	■	■	■				■		
		■			■	■	■	■	■			■	5	←
→	4	■				■	■	■				■		
		■					■					■	3	←
	2	■										■		
		■	■	■	■	■	■	■	■	■	■	■	1	

The bottom right corner is where you should start working, and Row 1 should be read from right to left. The information in Row 2 is read from left to right. You should start at the bottom of the chart and work your way up, reading the odd rows from right to left or the even rows from left to right as you go.

CONCLUSION

If you've never tried crocheting before, you may be curious whether it's a worthwhile hobby and whether or not you have the necessary skill set to get started. Does one need a certain level of skill to crochet?

The answer to that question is NO! There is absolutely no need for any specialized ability. You most likely already possess the necessary skill set as well.

The encouraging thing is that almost anybody can learn to crochet. Crochet is done by individuals of all ages, from very small toddlers to elderly people. Both women and men crochet. People from all over the globe do crocheting. Crocheting is a craft practiced by persons with impairments, including the blind. Everyone, regardless of socioeconomic status, crochets at some point.

You won't have a hard time getting started crocheting since there aren't many obstacles standing in your way, but there are a few things you should think about before you begin.

During times of conflict, it was standard practice for groups of individuals to work together to make clothes and other things, which were subsequently given as gifts to service members.

The creation of textiles using yarn and a single needle with a hooked edge is the practice of crocheting, which is a kind of yarn art. Crochet, much like knitting, may be used to make things like shawls, sweaters, and socks, among other things.

At first, crocheting and knitting were regarded as little more than leisure activities for folks with a lot of time on their hands. It was also a well-liked pastime for senior citizens, who would put their spare time to good use by sewing garments for their families and friends.

Nevertheless, as time went on, the tendencies shifted. Crocheting is becoming popular among people of all ages and provides an almost unlimited variety of project options. You did read that sentence correctly. Everyone of any age may give crochet a try.

Currently, it is possible to crochet almost anything and anything. After devoting yourself to mastering this craft and being familiar with at least three to four fundamental crochet stitching methods, you will be able to create various products using either a single stitch or a combination of numerous stitches.

We can divert our attention away from whatever has been giving us trouble by engaging in creative activities like crocheting and allowing ourselves to be spontaneous. The mind can become more peaceful and freer from nervous notions and thoughts when the person focuses on the repeated actions of individual stitches and counting rows.

Dopamine is a neurotransmitter that is produced in our brains when we engage in activities that we find enjoyable. This chemical affects our feelings and acts as a natural antidepressant.

Crafting, like crocheting, is thought by some researchers to have the power to improve our mood and make us feel better about ourselves. In this book we learned how to start crochet and learned its techniques and projects, we hope you enjoyed it.

Made in the USA
Las Vegas, NV
21 November 2022

59836068R00090